CrimeFighters: Retail Theft

Training Ordinary People to be Everyday Heroes

Vic Sellers

© copyright 2015 by Victor Sellers, CrimeFighters Press,
Los Angeles CA
New Castle PA
www.CrimeFightersUSA.com

CrimeFighters Press is a division of CrimeFighters USA, your partner in the battle against retail theft. CrimeFighters USA provides essential training for loss-prevention personnel, retail managers and small business owners, in the areas of detection, apprehension, prosecution, and safety instruction.

Cover design by Vila Design. Illustrations by Joby Harris. Photography by Lise Sentell and Dave Piesik. Editing by Mary Cameron and Nic Nelson. Interior layout and formatting by Wordsmith Writing Coaches.

ISBN-10: 0692630236
ISBN-13: 978-0692630235

This is dedicated to all the Store Detectives who worked with me and for me.
There are too many of you to mention. I won't put names here for fear of leaving someone out. The success we had in those stores was because of your hard work and the teamwork we exhibited. Thank you to each one of you. Your past efforts have been and will continue to be a constant inspiration to me and to my endeavors in the Loss Prevention field. If this book bears any fruit, it will be due largely to you.

Table of Contents

Preface

Loss Prevention requires taking responsibility to protect your assets, your merchandise, your customers and your employees! If you are the owner or manager of a store, then you are in charge of Loss Prevention until you hire someone for that role. If you have been hired for that role, you are the front line of defense to protect that retail business from being bled to death by shoplifting and other forms of theft. **CrimeFighters: Retail Theft** will help both of you succeed.

This book has grown out of many years of training, experimentation, failure and success. I want to save you the time and hassle of going through that years-long process yourself, and hand you all that accumulated wisdom in a single book, an operations manual for the store detective, and for anyone who needs to function like one.

A special thanks to the following police departments whose assistance was immeasurable while making my apprehensions:

> Baden Police Department
> Butler City Police Department
> Butler Township Police Department
> Cranberry Township Police Department
> Natrona Heights Police Department
> Ross Township Police Department

Acknowledgements

I wish to thank the following people for all their assistance in producing this training manual, my initial foray into the writing field. Along with their help it took a lot of thought, lots of midnight snacks and many nights in front of the computer to finally get it done. I can't believe it's actually completed. Hopefully there will be more to come. Thank you all!

Joby Harris – For the illustrations he designed, and his constant inspiration.

Joseph Zurynski – For everything he taught me on the job, whether it was related to internal or external theft. He was then and continues to be a great example and a great friend. Thank you Joe!

Mary Cameron – For her expertise with the initial editing and rewrites of the first draft of this book.

Tony Calaf – For keeping me going through the first few years of writing, as a business & life coach.

Marty Stahl and the staff of **Volunteers of America** – For helping me get this project off the ground during the initial phases.

Nicolas Nelson, my Editor – Through his many emails, phone calls, and rewrites, we were able to put this manuscript together. I may not have agreed with him on all the corrections, additions, and deletions, but in the end he has been instrumental in getting out the message I want to deliver.

CrimeFighters: Retail Theft
Training Ordinary People
to be Everyday Heroes

Introduction

Loss Prevention – It's a common term thrown around in retail circles. But what does it really mean?

A company I once worked for defined Loss Prevention as "controls and procedures designed to build an effective defense against all situations which may cause the loss of business assets and create inventory shortages." Granted, building an effective defense is important. But it's more than that. Loss Prevention is primarily taking responsibility to protect your own store! To protect your assets, your merchandise, and your employees! If you are the owner or manager of a store, then you are the one in charge of Loss Prevention for that store. And if you are a plain-clothes store detective, you are the front line of that defense, responsible for stopping the bleeding.

So how do you take charge and start protecting your livelihood?

You learn how the thieves do it. You learn observation techniques that will give you an edge. And once you learn how the thieves are stealing from you and how to watch them, you will be able to catch them with the goods.

You also learn how to apprehend them, legally and safely. You learn how to recover concealed merchandise, identify the shoplifter, and decide whether you want to file criminal charges against them. You learn ways to make your local police officer's life much easier, becoming an unofficial but effective partner with them as they strive to reduce crime in your store's neighborhood.

Fighting shoplifting is a team effort. It starts with you and your store's employees, but only fully succeeds when you work alongside the local police department and the courts to prosecute and convict those who shoplift. That is the only way to tackle the shoplifting problem that is not only plundering your store, but continues to plague our society today.

As long as there are stores with merchandise to steal, shoplifting will always be with us. It will never be totally resolved. But it can be confronted, discouraged, and dramatically reduced, if the store owner or manager or loss-prevention specialist will take firm and consistent action. You won't prevent shoplifting by doing nothing: by hoping it won't happen to you, or by pretending it really isn't a problem. You won't be able to prevent it by just scaring the thieves away either. The bad guys will just keep coming back, reassured that you are all bark and no bite. Unless you take an aggressive approach and go after the thieves, you can only delay, not decrease, your losses.

I can teach you how to stop them.

This book was written for both the inexperienced (who will definitely learn the basics) and the experienced (who will add to their knowledge). My hope is that by learning the proven methods in this training manual, you will be convinced to do something to help take back our communities and our stores from the criminals who now feel they have free rein. That is what I hope to teach you and your staff, and the main reason why I wrote this book.

Chapter 1 – Who & What to Look For

I played a lot of football as a kid and teenager, mostly sandlot. I'll never forget those pick-up games every fall weekend. I have also watched football regularly on TV ever since Bart Starr and the Green Bay Packers won Super Bowl II. I watched it enough to feel I could be the offensive coordinator on a college or pro team today. Okay, maybe an armchair quarterback. But if there is one thing I have learned from all that football, it is that teams that lay back and try to protect a lead, or are afraid to lose, usually get beaten. Winning teams don't lay back. They stay aggressive and remain on the offensive.

What does this have to do with stopping retail theft?

I worked for many major retailers over my eighteen-year career. Most were good companies to work for, some not so good. But one company in particular stands out. They stand out because they gave up! Perhaps sales were slumping or they had legal issues, I don't know all the facts. They just decided they were no longer going to prosecute or even apprehend people for shoplifting. They directed their security personnel to just scare them away once they spotted a shoplifter.

We used to call that "burning" a shoplifter. It's when you simply allow the would-be thief to see you watching them, and hopefully scare them into dumping any merchandise they have on them before leaving the store. This method serves as a last resort when you feel you haven't seen enough to make the apprehension, and don't want to take a chance of making a bad stop. Sometimes burning a shoplifter will successfully result in recovering your merchandise, but this method should not be standard policy! If all you do is burn shoplifters, it won't take long before the thieves figure out that you're not going to stop anybody. And what's to prevent them from trying again until they do get away with it? Before long, you'll have even a bigger theft problem than you had originally. By the way, that company I referred to was bought out soon after and no longer exists. The point here is that they became defensive to the point they were afraid to take any risks at all, and in that posture, the other teams—the thieves—always win!

It's time to go on the offensive. Starting with simple observation techniques, two of my initial goals are to teach you *who* to look for and *what* to look for.

Knowing *"who"* to look for

Before you start looking, you need to know what kinds of thieves are out there. There are several main types that fit into two categories:

> **A. Amateurs** (teenagers, college students, the elderly, neighbors, co-workers)—usually working alone. Their motive is usually personal use.
> **B. Professionals** (refunders, drug addicts, con men) — sometimes working in teams. Reselling the merchandise for profit is the usual motive.

All shoplifters fall into these two categories. A possible third category would be a kleptomaniac, which is someone who steals compulsively without economic motive. Kleptomania, as defined by the Encyclopedia of Mental Disorders, is:

> *a complex impulse-control disorder characterized by a recurrent failure to resist stealing. It is often seen in patients who are chemically dependent or who have a coexisting mood, anxiety, or eating disorder. People with this disorder have an overwhelming urge to steal and get a thrill from doing so. The recurrent act of stealing may be restricted to specific objects and settings. People with this disorder usually exhibit guilt after the theft.*

In my eighteen years of retail theft experience, I may have encountered only one instance of this malady. And in that case I felt the person was only using it as an excuse. Don't get me wrong, it is definitely a legitimate condition. But your chances of running across someone with it are rare.

A. Amateurs - Amateur thieves will be your main source of shoplifting problems. They may include the neighbor down the street, a person from your church, local teens and even the elderly from the local nursing home.

The reasons why amateurs steal are as varied as the people you'll encounter. Sometimes it is an impulse theft from someone who wouldn't normally shoplift. They may have recently lost their job. They may tell themselves that they deserve or need this item. Or they may see theft as an adventure or challenge, fueled by peer pressure (likely for teenagers). They may be going through personal or marital upheavals. It's not always greed! Unless they are professionally diagnosed as the kleptomaniac mentioned previously, there is always an underlying reason for the theft.

B. **Professionals** - Amateurs may make up the biggest part of your problem numerically, but professional thieves are the ones that can hurt you the most, both financially and physically. You'll need to be careful because this type includes not only refunders and drug addicts, but con artists and their accomplices. They will work in teams and they know how to spot you before you can spot them. That's because one of them is usually working as the lookout. Whether you are a store detective or someone in management, after you've been beaten by them a few times, you will quickly learn that you really have to outsmart them to catch them. And by "beaten" I mean they were one step ahead of you the whole time. When dealing with professional thieves, you may need a partner if you want to catch them in the act, just to make things even. Professional thieves can also be dangerous, especially if they are desperate. Shoplifting is the easiest way to support a drug habit once an addict's job and savings are gone.

Professional thieves rarely keep the items they steal for themselves, but resell them at half the value and keep the money. Usually the money is used to buy illegal drugs. Typically the street value for stolen merchandise is 50% of retail, according to several thieves I have caught. That was for cigarettes. Other items may get a better or worse rate of return.

One way to tell whether someone is an amateur or a professional: when stealing an item in a plastic blister pack, an amateur will take the time (or waste the time) to remove the item from its original packaging. Their line of thinking is that if they get caught with it, we won't be able to prove it belongs to the store. A professional, or at least a thief who has done this before, will just keep the item in its original package when they conceal it. They won't waste time ripping it out of a package, which can be noisy, messy, and draw attention. Experienced thieves know what they want, and they want to get it quickly and get out just as quickly.

Also, amateurs are concerned with anybody (including other customers as well as store employees) who might be watching them. The more experienced thieves and professionals don't really care about other customers. They'll steal right in front of them because the general public is clueless, and they know it. They're looking for employees and specifically you, the store detective or member of management. You are the bad guy as far as they are concerned: the one who will stop them, the one who will prevent them from earning their living.

The Gender Principle

"When it comes to stealing, women are clever and men are simple." Not only are there differences between amateurs and professionals in the ways they steal and the reasons why they steal, there are also differences between men and women. Because of these gender-specific tendencies, men will often be easier to catch than women.

Clever Female example #1: A woman intent on stealing a few packs of cigarettes will usually begin by getting a shopping cart as if she intends to buy bulky things or lots of things. She may cruise an aisle or two before winding up at the cigarette display. After selecting three packs from the display, she will put them beside her purse in the basket section of the shopping cart. She continues shopping. Soon the cigarettes are moved to the other side of the purse. Which side they wind up on before they vanish will depend on whether she is right- or left-handed, how close to the aisle she is, the way the purse is designed to open, etc. She may even perch them on the top of the purse. From here they are easily concealed into the purse in one swift movement. But during the course of the shoplifting act, she may move them at least once, and maybe two or three times, before she feels comfortable enough to tuck them away quickly and smoothly without being seen. Often it won't matter whether she is alone in the aisle or not. She's not a real professional, but she has this little theft act of hers down pretty good, or so she thinks. The woman may continue shopping after this concealment, coolly going through the check-out process, paying cash for the few items she has decided to buy, confident that you will think she is a legitimate shopper.

Clever Female example #2: A young woman pushes an empty shopping cart into the electronics department. She goes to the back and spends a long time looking at TVs. She finally places a 19" TV into her shopping cart. She continues to look at other items until the clerk is busy ringing out someone else. At that time she pushes her cart with the TV out of the department and heads for the front of the store. She spends a lot of time near the front checkouts and eventually pushes her cart into an empty aisle without a cashier. She removes the chain blocking the aisle and waits for the right moment. When she feels the coast is clear, she simply pushes the cart with the TV through the checkout aisle and heads for the exit doors. As she walks past all the other checkouts she appears to be just another customer leaving with her purchase. This is a classic example of a walkout of a large expensive item by a shoplifter. She was careful, patient, and bold, all at the same time. And she almost got away with it.

Simple Male example #1: A man who has decided to steal a few packs of cigarettes won't usually push a shopping cart. While a woman may continue shopping after her theft, a man enters the store for usually one thing, and then leaves. He tries to act casual and go more or less directly to his target item, in this case, the cigarettes. He selects three packs from the display, but instead of continuing to shop, he immediately hunts for an unoccupied aisle where he thinks no one can see what he is doing. He conceals the target items within the first 30 seconds of taking them. And he puts them down the front of his pants! He stops, looks back, and shoves the target items down as far as they'll go, then continues on his merry way out the door. "Down the pants" is the most widely-used concealment spot for men, and the concealment will happen immediately after picking out the target item– almost without exception, for amateur male shoplifters. The guys really do make it easy for you. No deceptive stratagem, no sleight of hand.

Simple Male example #2: A man in his mid-20s wearing a set of work overalls walks into our department store. He heads over to the hardware section and looks at tools, specifically crescent wrenches. He finally picks out the one he wants. It is the biggest wrench we sold. It has to be close to a foot and a half long, encased in a blister pack that made it even larger. He must need this particular wrench pretty bad. And he really doesn't have a place to put it. By now you can guess where it goes. Yeah, down the front of his overalls, fetching up somewhere between his waist and his knee. It wasn't hard to keep up with him as I followed him out of the store; he walked with an obvious limp, unable to straighten out his leg. After I stopped him and brought him back into the store, I told him I was glad he didn't try to run. He definitely would have injured some part of his anatomy in the process.

Knowing "what" to look for

The Opposites Principle

The differences between how a customer acts in your store and how a shoplifter acts are what I refer to as the Opposites Principle. An ordinary customer might accidentally look and even act like a shoplifter, but a shoplifter will not look and act like a customer. They will try to at first, but they always give themselves away eventually. Take time to study people. Start noticing the following clues that may tell you that you have a potential shoplifter. In each of the following, the Opposites Principle applies:

> a. Sudden head-turns – As you walk past an aisle and look down it, the person shopping in the aisle quickly lifts up or turns their head to notice you. If they are about to conceal something, they are looking up to see if you are watching them. This person is either

nervous (why?), unusually vigilant, or up to
something. An ordinary customer will not act this
way.

b. A watchful eye – Same as the sudden head turns. If a
person is more concerned with watching other people
than the merchandise in front of them, there is
probably a reason. In most cases when someone is
stealing, their eyes will give them away. They want to
make sure no one is watching what they are doing. So
watch their eye movements, but try not to make eye
contact with a potential shoplifter. That will give you
away almost every time.

c. Look at what people are carrying – large purses,
empty bags, a coat over the arm. If you notice
someone entering your store carrying a large shoulder
bag that appears flat, that is a red flag. Odds are that
bag will "magically" fill up as this person shops
around your store. The same goes for someone
walking into your store carrying their jacket or coat
over their arm. If it is that warm outside, why didn't
they leave it in the car? Why carry it in? It is very easy
to slip something underneath that jacket or coat and
walk out with it.

d. Look at what people are wearing – Their clothing
should match the weather outside. I have seen
increasing numbers of people, mostly young, wearing
t-shirts and shorts, and even sandals on cold days, but
this isn't a security problem. It's the other extreme
you need to worry about. If someone comes into your
store wearing a long winter coat and it is warm and
sunny outside, keep an eye on that person. Besides
weather-inappropriate clothing, baggy clothing is also
a red flag, since merchandise can be easily concealed
in its folds and pockets.

e. Look at what is in their shopping cart – Again, notice
what kinds of items people have in their shopping
cart. If someone walks out of the electronics
department pushing a shopping cart with multiple

DVDs or CDs, follow them to make sure they go
directly to the checkouts. What you need to keep in
mind is the "flow of merchandise." If someone selects
an item, and places it in their cart or under their arm,
where do they go with it next? Do they go pay for it,
or do they continue shopping? Where is that
merchandise going? If it goes in any direction other
than where the checkouts are located, keep an eye on
it until you are certain this person isn't a thief.

The most important things that separate professional thieves from
amateurs not mentioned earlier are the high dollar value of items
they steal and the quantity of them they will try to get out of your
store. They will usually go for high-quality expensive merchandise
because they get a better return when they fence it. The following
is an actual case of professional thieves working as a team that
involved a shopping cart, the "flow of merchandise," and an
unusually high dollar amount of stolen items:

Professional Theft Case #1 – September 5, 1998 (Wal-Mart):

I first saw the subjects as they entered the store: a young male (late
teens to early 20s) and older female (early to mid 40s). I
recognized the female as someone we were on the lookout for.
They immediately walked back to the Infants Department and
selected a stroller that came in a box. They placed it in their
shopping cart and continued shopping around the store.

When they entered the Toy Department, they took the box out of
their shopping cart and placed it among the large boxed toys (Big
Wheels, tricycles, etc.). They removed the stroller from the stroller
box and set it aside, leaving the empty stroller box among the
other similar-sized boxed toys.

They left Toys with the shopping cart and seemed to shop as
usual, throughout the store. They selected the items they wanted,
put them in their cart, covered them up with an article of clothing,
and headed back to the empty stroller box they had left in the Toy
Department. Then they removed the items from the shopping cart
and placed them into the empty stroller box. Then they closed up
the stroller box and went to get more merchandise. They repeated
this process numerous times until they filled the stroller box. Once

the box was filled, they taped it shut with tape they had picked up from our stationary department. Then they walked away and left the store. I had already radioed one of the managers on duty about what was going on, and he affirmed he would be ready to back me up.

Ten to fifteen minutes later, another young male with an empty shopping cart approached the Toy Department and entered the aisle where the box stuffed with merchandise was still sitting. He acted as if he knew right away which item he wanted. He lifted up the stroller box and placed it in his shopping cart. He then proceeded to the front checkouts and since the box was sealed, the cashier had no reason to suspect that anything other than a stroller was inside. He paid for the presumed stroller with cash (under $40) and pushed the shopping cart with the stroller box out the front doors.

I checked with the cashier to verify how much he had paid, then followed the suspect outside. With the help of the assistant manager I had radioed earlier, we stopped him just off the front sidewalk and returned him and the shopping cart to the security office. The suspect offered no resistance and acted as if he had done nothing wrong. Police were called and the suspect was arrested and taken into custody. We were unable to locate the other two individuals who had loaded up the box.

The older white female was later identified as the head of a local shoplifting ring who paid young males to do her stealing for her. She would pay them a set amount for assisting her, then sell the stolen merchandise, apparently at local flea markets. The total value of merchandise recovered in this case was close to $4,000.00 …in one stroller box!

Follow the Indicators

In the previous example of professional shoplifting it was not only the quality of the items taken, but also the quantity that mattered. Imagine what a team of shoplifters could take out of your store in those huge shoulder bags some women carry? Or in a large garbage bag? I've had cases in which four leather jackets (value $400), and six jogging suits (value $600) had been carried out of a store in garbage bags. Both cases involved professional shoplifters working in teams.

The point is to notice the dollar value of items people are carrying, or pushing around in their shopping cart, as well as the quantity of items. High dollar items, whether large or small, will be the favorite target of professional thieves. Experienced shoplifters don't come into a grocery store and try to walk out with a large bag of cheap dog food or a 24-pack of toilet paper. Oh, I'm sure it's happened somewhere. No, instead they'll try to steal expensive steaks or seafood, pricey electronics, or cartons of cigarettes. Lots of them. The same thing goes for a department store (big-screen TVs, air conditioners) or a clothing store (expensive jeans).

Equally important is to notice when store merchandise is found out of its container or in the wrong aisle. As mentioned in the previous shoplifting example, an empty stroller box can be used for a high-dollar theft if the box is later used to conceal other merchandise. If we hadn't captured one of the thieves involved in that theft, we might have been looking for this missing "empty" box the next morning, only because we found an unboxed stroller left behind in an aisle. It could just as easily be a two-foot section of empty hangers found on a display rack, or a pile of price tags cut off and left on a fitting room floor. But it's noticing things like these that can teach you what's happening in your store, as you begin to recognize evidence left behind by the shoplifters.

We've looked at several examples of suspicious shopping practices to look out for:

A)   Quantity – **Large quantities** of items, whether they are expensive or not, should arouse your suspicions and warrant following that person.

B)   Price – **Anything small and expensive** should send up a red flag simply because of the ease of concealing something small.

C)   Size – **Big and pricey items**, whether hand-carried or in a shopping cart, always warrant a second look to ensure they are going through the checkout and not directly into the trunk of a customer's car.

D)   Flow – **Where are shoppers and merchandise going?** Pay attention to where items are normally stocked, and how people and merchandise normally flow through the store, so that you will recognize when something is out of the ordinary (like an infant stroller shelved among the Big Wheels, or merchandise in someone's possession going in the wrong direction).

Most of this is just good old common sense. Stay on the lookout for these specifics about who and what to look for, and you'll begin to notice that not all your customers are who they appear to be. Of course, an ordinary customer may exhibit some of these tendencies. It is usually a combination of several of these indicators that will tell you there is a potential shoplifter in your midst.

Chapter 2 – Eliminating Opportunity

What is the most important thing a shoplifter needs in order to commit retail theft? In a word, opportunity. To identify theft opportunities in your store, put yourself in the position of the shoplifter. What will he/she be looking for prior to their theft attempt?

- No clerks or other customers around to observe them
- No security cameras or security personnel present
- Expensive/portable merchandise displayed unprotected

Any and all of these are opportunities sought by potential shoplifters. You make your job easier if you eliminate these opportunities, or take advantage of the thief's perspective of opportunity. One way to look at opportunity from the thief's perspective is what I call...

The "Food on a Plate Principle."

I love backyard barbecues. The smell of the food while it's cooking on the grill is mouth-watering. Problem is, bugs like the smell of cooked meat too. Or potato salad, or whatever you put on the picnic table. What invariably happens when you put an open plate of food on an outside table? You invite every insect in the surrounding neighborhood to join you. Think of your merchandise as the "food on a plate" and the potential thief as the hovering insects. Just as you wouldn't put a plate of food on that picnic table uncovered, you shouldn't put expensive merchandise on display unprotected. Otherwise, you invite every dishonest person who walks past to help themselves to the banquet you have set before them. Find a way to secure it!

Surveillance - Red Zones

Location is key when minimizing theft opportunities. "Red zones" are the key areas to watch. Call them whatever you want. These are your high shrinkage areas where theft has been or is most likely to occur. It could be the leather coats. It could be the jewelry department. It is definitely the electronics department. It is wherever you are experiencing a high amount of shrinkage (theft or unaccounted-for merchandise). These are undoubtedly the areas in your store that you will want to concentrate on. For example, there would be days during the Christmas holidays, that I would spend half my day patrolling the electronics department. I would try to give everyone who entered that department a look, and try to evaluate their potential for theft. Other areas of the store can also be red zones, even though the merchandise itself is not expensive. Some clues to be on the lookout for:

a) Keep track of where empty packages are found. This will usually show where the concealments are taking place. About half of the empty packages are found directly where the merchandise is displayed. For example, in the Cosmetics aisle you will find empty eyebrow pencil packages hanging right where they are sold. You may also find the same empty packages in another part of the store. I found a lot of empty packages in the Domestics Department (kitchen & bedding), usually shoved between two comforters. You may also find other empty packages or clothing hangers there; that tells you it is a favorite place where thieves prefer to commit the actual concealment. They may have picked it up somewhere else in the store, but they carried it back here to open the package and take possession of it.

b) Anywhere you stock or display small high-priced items is a potential red zone. I'll use the electronics department again as an example, because of the DVDs, CDs, and similar merchandise available there. Since they are relatively small items, some thieves don't stop at taking one or two, they may take a dozen or so. All small electronics like USB drives should be in locked display cases or in close proximity to the cashier station.

c) Entrances and exits are probably the worst places to display expensive merchandise that is not secured. Keep unprotected items away from the front door or exit doors. Most "grab and run" thefts occur with unprotected merchandise placed too close to an exit door. This sounds like common sense, but you might be surprised to discover how few retail stores seem aware of this. Unless you want to spend your time near the front door all day, secure the items. Otherwise you are simply making the thieves' job easier by putting the items they want right near the exit they need.

d) You can also do periodic physical counts of specific items of merchandise, and continue that throughout the day. At the end of the day, you can compare the difference in items remaining to how many were actually sold, to determine how much, if any, theft of that item took place.

Surveillance - Physical Barriers

Just as the would-be thief is looking for an opportunity to steal, you should be looking not only for ways to reduce that opportunity, but also ways to clearly observe the theft act taking place. Part of this is giving the thief a sense of "false opportunity." You do that by putting a <u>physical barrier</u> between you and the person you are watching. Use the unique makeup of the store to your advantage, to create those physical barriers. The following three examples may give you some ideas:

<u>Example #1</u>: One of my previous jobs was providing surveillance for a drug store in a small shopping center. There were a couple of back aisles where a lot of shoplifting was occurring. At the rear of the store was a display wall of merchandise. Behind that wall was a stockroom. In this type of commercial development, most wall construction consists of two layers of drywall about 3 to 4 inches apart. On the outside of that wall (the sales-floor side) was the pegboard that displays the merchandise. I simply cut a small hole on the outside layer of drywall and a bigger hole on the inside layer (big enough to get my eyes close enough to see through the pegboard on the other side). I could have moved the peg hooks on the outside to improve my view from the inside, but in this case it wasn't necessary. Unless there is a light on in the stockroom you are in, there is no way thieves will see you, and they will have a false sense of opportunity believing no one is watching them. You will now be able to observe the theft and concealment of

merchandise from behind your physical barrier (a wall), without alerting the thief to your presence.

DIAGRAM #1
DRYWALL BEHIND STOCKROOM

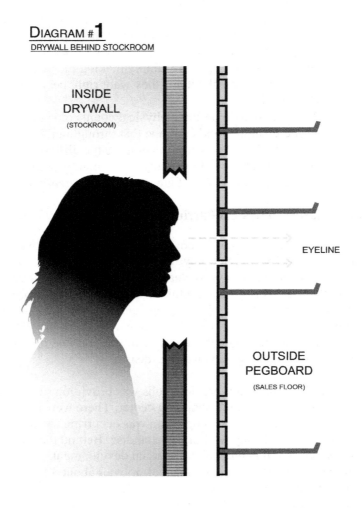

INSIDE
DRYWALL
(STOCKROOM)

EYELINE

OUTSIDE
PEGBOARD
(SALES FLOOR)

Example #2: A male and female shopper were identified as potential shoplifters by their suspicious actions. They were on a part of the sales floor that was fairly open with no fixed location to observe them from without being seen. They were standing behind a round display (a "rounder") of clothing items. The only way I could see what they were doing would be to get as close to them as I could. I was able to crouch down and get on the inside of another rounder approximately twenty feet from them. From inside that rounder of clothing, and peering out from between the coats that were on it, I was able to see one of the subjects pull out a garbage bag and open it up, while the other removed a handful of items from the rack (six jogging suits) and dropped them into the garbage bag, hangers and all. From behind those coats and inside the rounder, I was able to see the complete theft of merchandise (the taking and concealment) and was not spotted.

Example #3: As you walk the sales floor, you'll be surprised at the number of physical barriers you can construct throughout the store, sometimes on a daily basis. For example, most discount department stores, drug stores, and grocery stores have "end caps" that display merchandise at the end of an aisle. I have caught numerous shoplifters while watching them down an aisle from behind these end caps, when they assumed they were alone and unobserved.

Let's say a customer has just picked up several sets of expensive ear buds and leaves the Electronics Department. He or she walks to another part of the store and turns into an aisle where merchandise is displayed on the end cap. If boxes of merchandise are stacked there, simply arrange them so you have a small opening to peer through. You may feel your heart race as you observe the shoplifter look up and down the aisle, then shove the ear buds into a purse or backpack. Your adrenaline should be pumping every time you witness a shoplifter in the act. Take a deep breath and relax. The shoplifter won't notice you watching from behind the boxes. And the best part is, you are just around the corner, not stuck in an observation perch. There is no chance of losing visual contact with them or failing to catch up with them as they leave the store.

If the end cap has items hanging on peg hooks similar to the back wall in example #1, remove a few of the hooks with merchandise. By putting your eye up against a peg-hole opening, your field of vision opens up so that you can see the entire aisle. And they aren't going to look down the aisle and see you through a hole that is maybe a quarter-inch wide. Now a customer may walk by and notice you, but at this point you need to be able to concentrate on the shoplifter and not worry how many other people see you. (Just as professional thieves don't worry about whether customers see them conceal merchandise, professional store detectives don't worry about whether customers see them observing other shoppers in strange ways.) Once again, you have put a physical barrier, in this case the end cap, between you and the shoplifter.

DIAGRAM #2
LINE OF SIGHT: *SEEING THROUGH PEGBOARD AT AN ENDCAP*

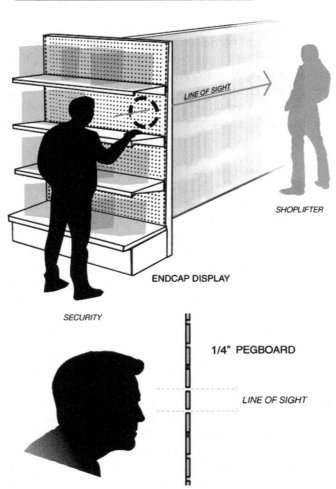

LINE OF SIGHT

SHOPLIFTER

SECURITY

ENDCAP DISPLAY

1/4" PEGBOARD

LINE OF SIGHT

A physical barrier may, as mentioned above, simply be some display boxes arranged to enable you to see behind them. It can be anything; even the phony shopping cart you may push around can be used as cover. All you need is a small opening to observe and watch the shoplifters through. Once again, I want to remind you to avoid eye contact with the subject.

Sometimes you will need to walk past the potential shoplifter to identify the specific items you think they are going to steal. You will want to know how many items they have and where are they located in the cart or basket. But as you do this you cannot look at them. Look past them, or through them, anything but directly at them. Because you can bet that if you walk down the same aisle they're in, they are looking at you to try to figure out if you are security.

Sometimes while walking past an aisle where a shopper has their back to you, you may hear what sounds like someone opening up a package. Learn to use your ears to listen for distinct sounds like the sound of plastic being cut, broken, or torn open. This probably won't be enough to base a stop on, but it will alert you to get yourself into a position to see what is going on. They might be opening a candy or gum wrapper from inside their purse or pocket, so it could be completely innocent. Or they could be removing an item from its outer packaging before concealing it. As soon as you think there is a theft taking place, concentrate on their hands. The eyes may give away their intent, but the hands do the stealing and that is what you need to watch.

Surveillance - Acting as Another Shopper

Dressing the part is also important when walking the sales floor, trying to keep an eye on all those customers. You have to blend in with the crowd. Remember, the job description is "Plain Clothes Detective." That means nothing that will make you stand out or be noticed. Favorites of mine were an old denim jacket and ball cap, or a hooded sweatshirt and a vest. The jacket and vest came in handy for the pockets to hold my ID, note pad and cuffs. The outer wear also comes in handy if it's nasty weather outside. You may have to dress down from what you are accustomed to wearing. But you'll be thankful, after you experience your first physical encounter, that you weren't wearing your favorite leather jacket.

Add to your security wardrobe a pair of jeans and a good pair of running shoes and you're all set! If you're a member of management and have to dress up, have an old jacket nearby that you can throw on when you need to. And take off the tie!

Earlier I referred to using a shopping cart as cover. It can also be your best prop as you pretend to be just another customer shopping in the store. Female detectives definitely have an advantage here. They can place their purse (where they can carry a radio, note pad, handcuffs) in the upper basket of the cart along with a few other items from the shelves as if they were shopping. Male detectives can push a shopping cart around, too, and look legit doing it. I call it the "lost husband look." You can even carry a phony shopping list and appear to be searching for some elusive item. This has worked for me on many an occasion. Even if you decide not to push around a shopping cart, you should at least carry around an item or two to make it look like you are shopping. Vary your props from day to day.

The whole acting part is essential if you don't want thieves to be able to spot you. You've got to be able to watch your suspect without attracting attention from other shoppers nearby. But when the critical moment arrives, the "moment of truth," you cannot be concerned with other shoppers or how you appear. You have to concentrate on the theft act, so you know exactly what is being concealed and where. Did the makeup items go into her purse, or into a coat pocket? Did that mini socket set go down the front of his pants, or did he pass it off to someone else? At this point, don't worry about other shoppers. Watch your suspect and watch their hands and don't take your eyes off of them. Even if you have to lie on the floor in the middle of an aisle – which I've done – you need to be able to see what you have to see.

Surveillance - Maintaining Visual Contact & Bad Stops

Surveillance may begin by watching the suspect conceal your merchandise, but it doesn't end there. What happens next after you have witnessed a concealment of your merchandise? For some, this may be the hardest part. Now you have to follow that person for as long as it takes until:

a) They put the item back because they changed their mind

b) They go to the checkouts, pull it out, and pay for it
c) They leave the store without attempting or intending to pay for the item or items.

In order to do this, you must maintain <u>100% visual contact</u> with the subject. If you lose them or they get out of your sight for any length of time, you cannot be certain they still have the merchandise where you saw them conceal it. If this happens, you should not stop the suspect. You don't want to make what is referred to as a "bad stop."

What constitutes a "bad stop?" This can occur anytime you approach someone, identify yourself as store security or store management, and return them to the store under the suspicion of shoplifting. If they don't have any of your store merchandise with them or on their person, you have just made a "bad stop" and can now be liable for false arrest, harassment, or any number of other charges. You will also have to explain to your supervisor what went wrong and the consequences related to that. That is why it is so imperative you follow the guidelines I have set out for you in this training manual.

Even if you do lose them for a second or two, you can ask yourself, "Have they had the opportunity to dump the merchandise?" If not, then you haven't really lost the chance to make a stop. Also, you may only see them conceal one or two items out of multiple items they stole. Maybe you watch someone place items 1, 6 and 9 out of ten things she puts in her purse. All you have to see is one. Even though you didn't see the other items that were concealed, you'll be able to recover them with the ones you did see. And I'll tell you how when we discuss processing the shoplifter in Chapter 6.

Chapter 3 – CCTV and Observation Windows

Using Observation Windows/Perches

One of the best tools I've had the privilege of using during my career are "security perches" or observation windows. The windows use panes of mirror-finish one-way glass mounted near the ceiling, and are designed so you can look out over the sales floor while no one on the sales floor can see you. I can't tell you how many thieves I've caught by watching them from one of these windows. Armed with a good pair of binoculars, you can practically put yourself right in their front pocket or purse, along with the merchandise they just concealed. Almost any store with a back room or stockroom can have a modest security perch and one-way window put in. For any business on a limited security budget, this could be your answer.

Most of the older discount department stores had plenty of these windows, usually on the back wall, which is where the main stockroom was located. If the store had an upper level in that stockroom, it was ideal for going from window to window to follow a suspect. You just had to keep an aisle clear along the wall, so you could get to the next window. We used to keep folding chairs at most windows with binoculars at strategic locations. Of course, in order to see down the aisles, the windows had to be aligned with the aisles in the store. See Diagram 3 below:

DIAGRAM #3

SECURITY WINDOWS OVERLOOKING THE BACK AISLES

Ideal conditions

For these one-way windows to work properly, they require darkness on the side you're on. Remember that these windows appear to be mirrors, but if there is light directly behind you, or the stockroom you're in is lit up, thieves can actually look up and see you. They may not be able to make out who is behind the mirror.

But they will be able to see a silhouette or the shadow of your head. At one retail location, after seeing a few shoplifters look up at us in the windows, we went down to the sales floor to figure out what they were seeing. What they saw was us, looking down on them. The normal stock room lights were giving us away.

Any light is bad and may give you away. So, when looking out one of these windows, try to stand off to one side when watching someone below. Avoid putting your face in the middle of the glass. That way, just in case they look up, they won't see an image or shadow of a face looking down upon them. One way to maintain appropriate darkness on your side of the window is by hanging a dark-colored cloth or curtain to shield the window from any ambient stockroom light. Or you could enclose the window in a small booth and have a dark room from which to look out and observe. Later, I'll discuss a simple way to install one of these windows.

Placement of windows

The placement of the windows depends on the merchandise you want to watch. If you have the luxury of placing or installing these windows yourself, you will want to place them to overlook the store's red zones where high-priced merchandise is displayed, or near any merchandise that is prone to theft. They should also be placed anywhere you are unable to monitor a particular area with a camera or from the floor without being conspicuous. Ideally, for maximum coverage, you want a window placed every two or three aisles. This way, as the subject moves, you can simply move to the next window to maintain visual contact with them, as you near your exit point to return to the sales floor. This is important because you absolutely must be...

Maintaining visual contact!

Just as the location of windows to the proximity of your expensive merchandise is important, so is easy access into and out of these observation areas. They need to be close to stockroom or office doors or stairways, for quick entry and exit. If you observe someone conceal merchandise from a window, you will have to leave that window to return to the sales floor. When you do, you have now lost sight of the subject and failed to maintain 100% visual contact, and you cannot stop the suspect unless and until you are certain the merchandise is still concealed on them or with them.

After leaving the window to re-enter the sales floor, you should only stop a shoplifter under the following conditions:

a) You are working with a partner who can pick up the visual surveillance from the sales floor after you witness it from the window. A pair of radios would come in handy for this.

b) It is obvious to you that the merchandise you saw concealed, still is! This would depend on its location or placement on the subject. For example, a shoulder bag they stuffed full of items is still full.

c) The subject has had no opportunity to "dump" or discard the merchandise. Maybe there are just too many customers around. The thief is not going to dump items that have been concealed unless something has scared them. Unless they spotted you, they most likely still have it concealed.

Even if you have to let them walk because you are not absolutely certain, you now know what they look like. They'll be back, and you'll be waiting for them.

Binoculars

As I mentioned earlier, try to keep a decent pair of binoculars handy. You'll need them whenever the subject isn't directly beneath you. You don't need one at every window (unless you can afford it), but maybe spread them out so that one isn't too far away when you need it. And remember where you last left them. You don't want to get to your window location, not be able to find the binoculars in the dark, and possibly miss a concealment you should have seen. A pair of 10x50 binoculars works perfectly for getting up close so you can see what you need to see.

The Flow of Merchandise

In Chapter 1 I talked about the "Opposites Principle." One facet of this principle is the flow of merchandise. If you remember, there are differences in how an ordinary customer and a shoplifter will act. In this instance, shoppers select an item they want and take it to the checkout area to purchase it. Thieves will also select an item they want, but will usually take it to one of the rear aisles of the store so they can conceal it. They go to the back of the store because there are usually less people there. If you are watching over an area from an observation window at the back of the store, you may see them bring the item they want right to you, and conceal it right under your nose. If you are working the sales floor and someone walks past you pushing a shopping cart with multiple expensive items, or simply carrying them, follow your merchandise to make sure it gets paid for. Again, whether you are working the floor or observing from a window, watch the direction the merchandise flows.

How to install an observation window

By following the four-step process and diagrams shown here, we will have you watching over your sales floor in no time. After you select the area of the store you want to observe, you need to pick the best vantage point for the observation window. As well as giving you the best view of the department, this observation window also has to be accessible from a back office or stockroom. Remember, this window should be near the ceiling. If there is no second-floor area behind that window where you can sit and watch, you may end up building a landing or platform. Make it big enough to fit a chair for you to sit in as you watch out the window. The platform only needs to be strong enough to hold your weight. Unless you're a carpenter, hire a professional to build this for you. You want to be safe going into and getting out of that perch, since you'll be doing it often.

DIAGRAM #4
STOCKROOM PLATFORM WITH RAILING

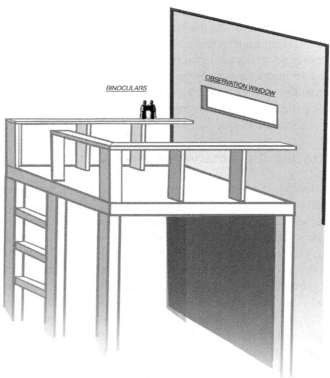

INSIDE BACK STOCKROOM

Step 1 – Frame: Select your frame for your observation window. A simple 8"x11" picture frame will work perfectly. It should be made of wood so you can drill holes into it.

Step 2 – Glass: You can get one-way mirrored glass at your local glass distributor. Remove the original glass from the frame and insert your one-way glass. Use tacks or small nails to hold it in place since you can't use the backing.

Diagram #5

OBSERVATION WINDOW INSTALLATION

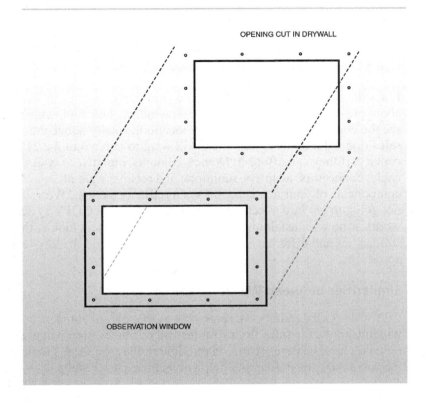

OPENING CUT IN DRYWALL

OBSERVATION WINDOW

Step 3 – Drywall: Select your location, measure the inside of the picture frame, and cut the opening in the drywall to match the inside of the picture frame. I use a jigsaw to make the opening. You'll have to make a small hole first to get the jigsaw blade through. Pound a couple nails through, just big enough to start your jigsaw. Once your opening matches your inside frame, you are ready to install your window. Insert your picture frame from the outside. Use screws or nails to hold it against the drywall.

Step 4 – Booth/Curtain: It has to be dark on the observer's side for these windows to work best. So, either arrange for the store employees to leave the lights off in that area while the store is open for business, or arrange for some way to block any light from reaching your vantage point and the backside of that mirrored window (such as hanging a dark colored curtain over the window).

Use of CCTV (Closed-Circuit Television)

Enter the electronic age. In this chapter so far, we've been talking about pre-camera systems: observation windows and being able to see the concealment from an on-site location, usually above the sales floor. But many storeowners will want to move into the 21st century, if they can afford it. Domes, cameras, mounts, coaxial cable, connectors, adapters, monitors, and receivers are all components of your average CCTV surveillance system. We're not going to get into a technical discussion of how a CCTV system works or how to install one. But we are going to take a look at the similarities and differences between the high-tech and the low-tech approach.

Similarities between Windows and Cameras:

CCTV works essentially the same way as that old mirrored window above the sales floor. But instead of observation windows now you have cameras scattered throughout the store. Let's look at the ways they are similar and help you get the same results.

- A camera puts you in the same aisle as the shoplifter with no chance of being seen, just like the windows. A shoplifter will ignore a camera the same as he would ignore an observation window. He assumes there is no one watching, so he steals anyway.
- Cameras are usually above the specific department and near the ceiling, just like the windows. With a camera though, you can hide it in a dome, although the dome will still be visible. A shoplifter won't know whether the camera is pointing at him, or if there is even a camera in that dome or not.
- You can have dummy cameras and domes the same way you can have dummy windows, to discourage theft in

certain areas, or to fool shoplifters into turning toward
your actual observation vantage point (while they turn
their backs toward the more obvious dummy camera or
dummy window).

- With a camera system, you will still have to run to the
  security/control room to watch the thieves on the monitor.
  This is just the same as running to get to the window
  location in time to watch the theft.
- The zoom lens on your surveillance camera works like
  your pair of binoculars in the window. It allows you to see
  up close just what their hands are doing.

It takes at least two persons working together for CCTV to be an
effective tool: one to watch the monitor, work the camera(s) and
maintain 100% surveillance of the subject, plus a second security
person on the sales floor whom you can advise via silent texts or a
two-way radio. If you are working the sales floor, you are
reporting (via that 2-way radio or text messages) suspicious
persons and activities to the person working the camera(s). The
CCTV operator can then observe and even record a theft as it
happens, and guide the sales floor associate into position to make
the apprehension.

Differences Between Windows and Cameras:

It's hard to argue against technology. Just as there are obvious
similarities between the two systems, there are also obvious
differences. One is definitely superior to the other. Or is it?

- With the camera system, you can tape the theft for future
  use in court or for instruction. You can't do that with what
  you see from a window, all you have is your testimony
  from memory.
- The camera system usually takes two people as mentioned
  previously, unlike the window that needs just one. Unless
  your camera/control room is near the exit doors. Then, as
  you watch your thief approach the doors, you just prepare
  to step out and leave the store right behind him.
- Repairs and replacement of camera equipment. This is a
  biggie! Equipment being down for any length of time
  means you are trying to do a job with fewer tools in your
  toolbox. Sometimes you can move cameras around to

make up for those under repair. But even if you happen to have a spare on hand, you are going to spend at least some time and money replacing components. I don't ever remember an observation window breaking down.

- A camera system costs more. A lot more. A good system can range in the thousands of dollars. You can spend less. Either way, you will often be tempted to upgrade your system as new security tech is developed. Whether you choose a basic single-camera CCTV with pan/tilt/zoom, or a multi-camera multi-monitor CAT-7 network with all the bells and whistles, the benefits of your camera system should outweigh its costs, in terms of losses prevented over its useful life.

Budgetary constraints will usually determine just how expensive a system you can install in your store. And if you belong to a chain of stores, as opposed to being an independent, the decision probably won't be yours. Whichever system you have, or whatever budget you're on, you need to get a return on your investment.

"Spread the Butter" Principle

What does spreading butter on a piece of bread have to do with retail security? If you have toast for breakfast in the morning, you decide how much butter to put on that piece of toast, whether to lay it on thick, spread it thin, or somewhere in between. Perhaps you are on a diet and choose to keep it thin on principle. If you are on a tight budget and have to make one pat of butter last until the next grocery trip, you may have to spread that butter on that bread pretty carefully to reach all four corners. Regardless of how much butter you have, how do you spread it to give you the best coverage?

The same approach goes with the security budget for your business. Whether it's paying for a camera system or hiring detectives to monitor your store, you only have so much money to spend. Just like on that piece of bread, where you can only spread the butter so thin to be able to taste it, don't spread your coverage so thin that it doesn't have a chance to be effective. Depending on your specific business, you must allocate your resources to give you the best bang for your buck. A loss-prevention professional can show you how to identify and address the specific problems in your particular store, and where best to allocate your budgeted dollars.

Chapter 4 – Apprehension: Making an Arrest

Part I - The Three Elements of the Crime

Now that you know what types of suspicious behaviors to look for, and who you're looking for, we can now concentrate on the theft act itself. Unlike a police officer who usually arrives on the scene after a crime has been committed, then gathers evidence in the hope of making an arrest, you have to actually witness the crime as it is taking place. Then you make an immediate arrest based on what you have just witnessed.

There are certain acts that you simply **must** see an individual commit, before you can spring into action and place that individual under arrest. Different retail companies use different terms to refer to these acts: you may hear them called conditions, rules, or proofs. You can call them anything you want; I prefer to call them "elements." Also, every major retailer has a different number of them that has to take place before you make a stop: four rules, five proofs, six conditions and so on. The number is not important, just what they include. So for simplicity sake, I boil it down to three. Throughout the rest of this manual, these acts that must occur and must be observed by you will be referred to as "the elements of the crime." The three basic elements are as follows:

Element #1: The Taking
Element #2: The Concealment
Element #3: The Carrying Away

Let's break these three elements down one-by-one and look at exactly what you need to see in order to make a successful apprehension.

Element #1 - The Taking

"Taking" is when an individual selects an item of merchandise that is for sale in your store, and it is now in his or her control. This is an item or items you saw them select off a shelf or display, and that the individual now has in their control. They haven't purchased it yet, and they certainly don't own it, but they are carrying it in their hands or are pushing it in a shopping cart. So they now have control over that particular item or items they selected. And having control, they can do a number of things with that bit of merchandise. They can purchase it at the checkout counter, they can change their mind and leave it in some other part of the store, they can damage it in some way, or they can steal it. If it happens to be food, they can also consume it, which is the same as stealing it. Of all those choices, hopefully they will choose to proceed to a checkout and pay for it. If they are planning on stealing it, your job is to see when they take the next step.

Examples of The Taking:

> Scenario A: A female in her early twenties, with her purse over her shoulder, selects several items of makeup from the Cosmetics Department and carries them in her hand as she leaves the area.

> Scenario B: A male in his mid-forties walks into the Automotive Department pushing a shopping cart. He picks out a package of spark plugs, tosses them into his shopping cart, and pushes the cart out of the department.

> Scenario C: A male subject, mid-thirties, walks into the Electronics Department, chooses three DVDs, puts them under his arm and walks out of the department.

Obviously, not everyone who selects merchandise is going to end up stealing it. All three of the above examples may just be average customers coming into your store, finding what they came in for, and now they are going to a checkout to pay for it. They are here in your store to buy something. But you don't know whether they are customers or shoplifters unless you continue to watch them. One clue was how they went about choosing these items. Were they acting suspiciously as they did it? And what constitutes "acting suspiciously?" Let's see what else they did.

We'll back up those three scenarios just a bit. Even before the individuals selected any merchandise, certain things marked them as persons worth watching. Suppose you had observed the following behaviors prior to the Taking.

> Scenario A: The female shopper entering the Cosmetics Department is carrying a large purse that appears to be empty.

> Scenario B: The spark-plug-taker is more concerned with watching every other person in the Automotive Department than he is with inspecting the merchandise.

> Scenario C: When the mid-thirties male came in the front doors five minutes ago, grabbing a shopping cart and heading straight for the Electronics Department, you remembered seeing him in the store a week or so ago, doing the same thing.

Remember who and what to look for from the previous chapters. Suspicious behaviors prior to the Taking are pointers to a potential theft. In review, some of those suspicious behaviors are:

- Entering the store with large purses, shoulder bags, or backpacks that seem empty.
- Entering the store wearing baggy or weather-inappropriate clothing.
- Being more concerned with watching other people instead of looking at the merchandise.
- Making a quick head-turning motion or furtive glance with their eyes as you or other people walk by, to see if someone is watching them.
- Selecting merchandise almost indiscriminately, without examining things like size, style, or color. On one occasion I saw a man reach into a glass display cubicle and pull out half a dozen expensive sweaters and plop them in his cart. He never looked at any of the sweaters to check the sizes or colors. I knew right then I had a thief, because an honest person doesn't shop that way.
- Selecting expensive merchandise, or items particularly targeted for theft.

- Heading for a different part of the store after picking up an item, rather than heading for the checkout counter. Keep the "flow of merchandise" in mind. What direction is the merchandise going? If a person enters a fitting room with an armful of electronics instead of clothing, it is a pretty clear indication that a theft may be in process.

In most instances, customers may not have given any indication that they will steal anything. In fact, everyone who shops, customer or thief, will engage in this first element. Most people are legitimate customers who will continue shopping or proceed to the checkout area. Once you determine they're okay, you will just look for someone else to watch. When a person does give you an indication that they might proceed from simply Taking to Concealment by doing something suspicious, that's when you realize you've got a potential thief on your hands.

 The importance of seeing the first element of the crime, the Taking, is being able to identify the merchandise in question as belonging to your store. You must be sure it is not the customer's own item, something he brought into your store from another store, or an item that has already been paid for. When you know with certainty that it is store merchandise they are carrying because you saw the Taking of it, you can continue to observe them confidently. For example, a customer could have been emptying his pockets to locate something before you began observing him, and the item you see him pick up and conceal in his pocket may be his own wallet, his own camera, or his own cigarette lighter.

There are lots of different scenarios we could look at, but let's examine one actual incident that will show you the importance of consciously noting all three elements of the crime. The following example started out innocently at first, like most do. But it soon developed from just a potential shoplifting into a multiple-shoplifter scenario and arrest.

Test Case – Conspiracy Part One

A couple in their thirties enters a large department store in a popular mall and proceeds to the Men's Department. The female shopper selects several expensive sweat suits from a display rack.

She is calm and does not seem overly vigilant, not giving any obvious indication she may be a shoplifter. She simply hands the items to her boyfriend as she continues shopping. Again, all we have seen so far is a young couple shopping at the mall. They have done nothing more than take merchandise off a display rack. But that is just when things begin to get interesting!

Remember that all three elements of the crime **have to occur and be observed** in order to make an apprehension. Many potentially suspicious signals accompanied this Taking. First, the cost of the items taken: the sweat suits go for $100 apiece. Second, the quantity of the items taken: she handed a total of six sweat suits to her boyfriend, more than a shopper would normally take all at once… especially without even a glance at colors or sizes, which was the third suspicious signal. Fourth, since it is clothing, and pricey clothing at that, a typical next step for a serious shopper would be to try them on. But these two never look for a dressing room. Finally, as the female shopper was picking out the suits, her boyfriend was looking around to see if they were being watched.

By selecting and taking control of the items, our female shopper committed the Taking. But now we have suspicious behavior to go along with the first element of a potential crime. It all starts with the Taking: how, where, and when are less important than what is taken, and especially the behaviors that point to why it is taken. Now let's move on to concealing the merchandise.

Element #2 - The Concealment

What constitutes a Concealment of merchandise? To conceal is to hide from view. Concealment takes place when the individual that selected merchandise in your store then **hides it from view** on their person, in something they are carrying or controlling, or someplace else in the store. They might or might not remove the price tags or packaging before concealing it: whether they do or not doesn't change anything. If they do, it will just verify sooner their intention to shoplift. By concealing the item, they have more than simply taken control of an item; they have taken possession of it!

In most jurisdictions, **criminal intent is established upon concealment of merchandise**. To prove intent, make sure you see them conceal it, and that you know exactly where it is they put it. Here are three observed concealments to illustrate this:

A. Three women, late teens to late twenties, while looking around to see if anyone was watching, selected multiple items of children's and ladies' clothing. They placed them into their shopping cart and proceeded to the rear of the store. By their suspicious actions and the flow of the merchandise it was highly probable that a theft was about to take place. That was confirmed as I entered a stockroom and was able to observe the subjects from behind the rear wall pegboard display. As they entered a back aisle in the Toy Department, they immediately began to remove the hangers from the clothing and conceal the clothing on their person and in their purses. They then hid the hangers among the toys on the shelf.

B. From a security window overlooking the Men's Department I observed a female subject in her late thirties remove four brand-name T-shirts off a display rack, take them behind a rounder (a round display rack for hanging merchandise) along the back wall, and re-hang them on that rounder. Again, the flow of the merchandise (moving the items from one rack to another less-visible rack) alerted me to a potential theft about to take place. I watched the subject pull a shoulder bag out from under her coat. She quickly removed the T-shirts from the hangers and placed them in her bag. She then turned around, took a pair of black pants off the rack just behind her, and placed it in her bag as well, without looking at its tags.

C. While walking through Housewares, I saw a male with several pairs of slacks in a shopping cart, bending over a new brown plastic garbage can, one of several on display. I went to the nearest observation window and observed him placing something in this same garbage can. After he left the area pushing the shopping cart, I went down to the sales floor, looked inside the garbage can, and saw there were cartons of cigarettes inside. I then watched him go to the register area where the cigarettes are stocked, place several cartons in his cart, cover them up with the slacks, then return and conceal them inside the garbage can along with the other cartons of cigarettes. I watched him make this trip three times. He finally came out of the Rubbermaid aisle pushing the cart with the new garbage can inside. He pushed it past the middle of the store and was approaching the exit when several accomplices came in from outside and warned him that he was being watched. He walked away from the shopping cart and left the store. We counted 58 cartons of cigarettes inside that garbage can. (This was before cartons of cigarettes were displayed in locked showcases.)

Test Case – Conspiracy, Part Two

We left our two shoppers walking through the Menswear Department, she still looking at clothing racks, he carrying the "Taken" sweat suits. I watched them from my position underneath a rounder approximately twenty to thirty feet away. At this point, a shopping bag with handles emerged in one of their hands. With them standing side by side, I could see the bag unfold, but it was difficult to tell which of them unfolded the bag. Nevertheless, six silk sweat suits were then placed into the handled bag, hangers and all. Both subjects then left the department with the male subject carrying the very full shopping bag.

It really doesn't matter which of them placed the items in the bag, or which one was holding the bag as the items were dropped in, or who pulled out the bag and opened it up. In this case, because they actively worked together, our two subjects both took part in committing the Concealment of store merchandise. We have clearly witnessed the second element of the crime. And we also have the opportunity to apprehend a pair of shoplifters, not just one.

As a Concealment of merchandise takes place, especially if it is witnessed first-hand (but also if it can be logically inferred— although that allows room for argument) a potential crime turns into a clearly-defined theft. Now let's move on to the Carrying-Away, the third element.

Element #3 - The Carrying-Away

According to the Pennsylvania Crimes Code, Section 3929(a), a person is guilty of retail theft if he/she:

takes possession of, carries away ...any merchandise displayed, held, stored or offered for sale...with the intention of depriving the merchant of the possession, use or benefit of such merchandise, without paying the full retail value thereof.

For Element #3, we will concentrate on the last phrase "without paying the full retail value thereof." What does that entail? To pay something less than the full retail value usually means the subject left the store without paying anything for the item in their possession. The item might be concealed or not concealed, as you will see in the examples below. But they **do** need to remove it from the store, **past the last point of sale**. For without Element #3, a crime has not yet been committed, even if the intent to do so is already established by Element #2. Some state laws may differ, allowing you to stop them in the store once you witness a Concealment of merchandise. But if you want to win an airtight case in court, you need to let them walk out of the store before making the apprehension. Here are three examples of the Carrying Away:

A) As I mentioned earlier, the item doesn't always have to be concealed. We had just opened a Wal-Mart store less than a week earlier when I noticed a young female subject pushing an empty shopping cart as she entered the Electronics Department. She removed a boxed 19" TV from a shelf towards the rear of the department, placed it in her shopping cart and left the area. She proceeded to the front checkouts pushing the shopping cart, an encouraging sign of the flow of merchandise. But she entered a checkout line that was without a cashier, and slowly pushed her cart through. She pushed the cart past all of the registers **and walked right out the front doors without paying for the TV**. I approached her from behind, grabbing hold of the cart while she was still on the sidewalk, before she could reach her vehicle. I identified myself and returned her to the store without incident. In this instance, only two elements were needed to make a successful apprehension. No Concealment took place. This is called "a walkout," and it happens with the merchandise in plain view.

B) Wearing concealed clothing underneath your own and walking out of the store is a different method of the

Carrying-Away. A man was observed in Menswear selecting slacks from the rounder and jeans from the shelf against the wall. He carried the items along the perimeter wall, making his way to the men's fitting room, where he spent the next several minutes. Upon exiting the fitting room, his clothing was noticeably bulkier and the fitting room stall was empty except for two hangers and an empty shopping bag. We stopped him as he attempted to leave the store via the lower mall entrance. He offered no resistance as we escorted him to the Loss Prevention office. Once we got him there, he removed nine articles of clothing belonging to the store that were concealed on his person; the total value of the stolen clothing came to $392.98.

C) We observed a man in his mid-forties entering the store holding the side of his jacket as he came in, as if he was supporting something hidden inside. This tipped us off that he was a potential shoplifter. He entered Menswear as I entered the security perch overlooking that department. I could see the subject standing behind a sweater cubicle where he believed his next actions would be hidden from view. He pulled a brown garbage bag out from under his jacket and started placing sweaters from the cubicle into the bag. He immediately strode toward the nearest exit with bag in hand. As he entered the first set of doors into the foyer he spotted us following him, and started to run. I caught up and grabbed him from behind as he was going out the second set of doors. We tumbled onto the sidewalk outside as my partner radioed for the credit office to call the police. As I attempted to identify myself, he continued to struggle until I was able to wrestle him to the ground. My partner handcuffed the subject while I held onto him. He was cooperative once we returned to the Loss Prevention office. We recovered five sweaters valued at $460.00 from the garbage bag.

Test Case – Conspiracy, Part Three

Our male and female subjects had entered the Men's Department and stopped to look at expensive sweat suits. The female subject committed the first element of the crime (the Taking) by selecting the items from the display. Both subjects then committed the second element of the crime (the Concealment) by acting together in placing the sweat suits into a shopping bag.

Both subjects then headed toward the exit doors, although in a roundabout way. I followed and waited until the male subject walked out of the store with the shopping bag. I stopped him just as he exited the foyer onto the sidewalk, and identified myself as store security. He returned with me into the store without incident. The female subject, who had not left the store and probably witnessed the apprehension of her partner, attempted to hide in the women's restroom. A female store detective working with me apprehended her there.

By walking out of the store with the bag in his possession (containing the concealed merchandise), our male subject committed the all-important third element of the crime (the Carrying-Away). What's noteworthy about this case is that we were able to apprehend and prosecute both individuals. By the actions we witnessed, we were able to prove that not only did both have physical control over the stolen items at separate times, but by acting together, both were involved in committing all three elements of the theft act.

In most cases I have seen, when there is both a male and female involved, the female will usually walk out with the concealed merchandise, while the male will act as a lookout. That wasn't the case here, but it is something to keep in mind if this situation ever comes up in your store.

Part II - Apprehension Outside the Store

You've just witnessed a concealment of your store's merchandise. The subject is heading for the exit doors. You are the one who has to make the apprehension. Do you stop him now, or wait until he gets out the door? Why on earth would you want to wait until he steps outside and possibly gets away?

There are several reasons why you might want to wait and apprehend him outside the store:

- Company policy – Does the company you work for have guidelines regarding apprehending someone for shoplifting, such as the three elements that we are using, with the third element being the Carrying-Away? If so, you will have to make all apprehensions outside the store.
- Allow the shoplifter to <u>complete the theft act</u> – As mentioned earlier, and it needs repeating, if you want to ensure you can win this case in court, let them walk out the door before you make the stop. Just before I approach the subject to make the stop and identify myself, I ask myself this question: Can I win this in court if they choose to go to trial? If you allow the subject to complete the theft act by allowing them to do the Carrying-Away, you have taken away from them their best defense for failing to pay for the item. If you stop them in the store, they could always say they were planning to pay for it, but were not given the chance.
- Avoid premature stops – Of course, there is always the possibility that someone <u>was</u> actually going to pay for the item. I have watched people put merchandise in their pocket, technically committing a theft (depending on your state law), then pull it out at the register and pay for it. This especially happens with small inexpensive stuff. They may have concealed it from a fussy child who is with them, or they may have had their hands full and pocketing the item was just easier than trying to carry it. If you want to avoid an embarrassing moment for the customer, and for you, let them walk out of the store with it. Then, even if they did forget it was there, you've covered yourself in case store management prosecutes them and they choose to fight it in court.

This rule is particularly important when Element #2, the Concealment, has not taken place. Take the example of a flat screen TV in a shopping cart. You watched them put it in their cart, and then push it towards the front doors. But if they have not concealed or hidden it they have not demonstrated criminal intent, and you have no grounds to stop them— unless they push the cart and TV outside, past the last point of sale. It's the same when you see someone take a coat off the rack, drape it over their arm, and head for the doors. You can't stop them unless and until they walk out the door with it. In order to establish intent of theft without Concealment, you must wait until the Carrying-Away, when they remove the merchandise from your store.

Of course there are a few exceptions to this rule.

One exception is being overruled by the store manager. As a traveling detective, I was working in a grocery store and spotted a middle age couple concealing multiple packages of meat in a bag placed in the center of their grocery cart. The outside of the cart was lined with large items like cereal boxes and paper towels to block anyone from seeing the bag. I informed the manager about what was taking place, and he made the decision to stop them before they could make it to the exit.

Another exception is when the Taking involves vandalism. If a display case was broken into, a garment cord was cut, or a cash register was broken into, and the subject has the store merchandise (or cash) and is heading for the doors, you already have your criminal intent clearly established and can make the stop inside the store. We'll talk about "Smash and Grab" thefts in a later chapter.

Another is when the Taking is followed by consuming the product taken. You would think you would stop someone who consumed a food item in your store, then discarded the package. But when observing a customer consuming food items, I do not stop them, but continue watching them, knowing there is a good chance they will steal some other item, something inedible that they will then Carry Away. You may have the empty package to show they consumed the food in the store without paying for it, but without the physical evidence (the item now consumed) or clear video evidence, it's your word against theirs. Now that you know that person has the mindset of a thief, it's better to wait for a clean opportunity to stop and arrest them.

After all this due diligence, when you do move to apprehend the subject(s), here are some important points to keep in mind:

- All apprehensions should take place immediately outside of the exit doors. The further away from the store you are when you make the stop, the further you are from other employees, who might serve as backup. If you are out of view, there is no one watching your back. For your own safety, stop the subject as close to the entrance as possible.

DIAGRAM #**6**

CONFRONTING AND APPREHENDING

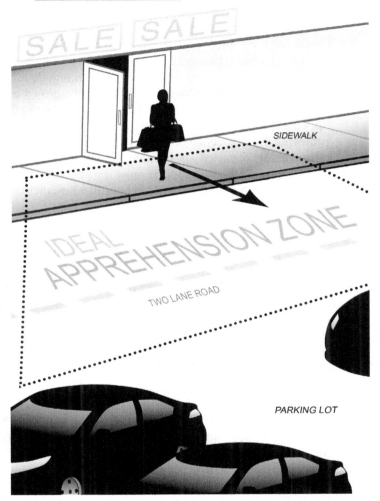

SIDEWALK

IDEAL APPREHENSION ZONE

TWO LANE ROAD

PARKING LOT

- Apprehend all subjects before they can get to their car. Attempting to pull someone out a car is not recommended (See "Top 10 Cases" numbers 2 & 7). While working in an Aliquippa, PA drugstore, I observed a woman conceal multiple cosmetics items in her purse and leave the store. By the time I could follow her outside, she had already gotten into the backseat of a car in one of the front parking spots. Approaching the vehicle, I immediately opened the left-rear car door, identified myself, and was able to talk the woman out of the car and back into the store. Even though it worked that one time for me, I would not recommend it as standard practice. Once the subjects make it to their car, just get the license plate number and call the police to report the theft.

- Apprehend the subject with a minimum of public disturbance. To some persons, you may not seem much of a hero, especially if you are a male apprehending a female and you have to march her back to the store through a crowd of people on a busy day. I had this happen to me once after apprehending a female in her late twenties who repeatedly protested her innocence on the way back in, to a crowd of onlookers who started questioning me as to why I stopped her. I shouted who I was to the most hostile onlooker, warned them not to interfere, and continued escorting her into the store.

If you get involved in a physical altercation with a shoplifter, it may invite other customers to involve themselves, however misguided, into breaking up "the altercation" and unwittingly assisting the shoplifter. Or they might intentionally side with the shoplifter; in that case you will have a problem. In one instance, a customer actually pulled me off a shoplifter whom we had just chased and brought down. He may have thought he was doing a good deed since my partner and I had this guy down on the ground. We still got the thief despite this customer's efforts to aid him.

Whatever his reasoning, he was in the wrong. But you, as the person making the apprehension, are in the right. And the Crimes Code in your state gives you that right. Let's look at the Pennsylvania Crimes Code as an example.

AUTHORITY: Pennsylvania Crimes Code, Section 3929(d): Detention - *A peace officer, merchant, or merchant's employee or an agent under contract with a merchant, who has probable cause to believe that retail theft has occurred or is occurring on or about a store or other retail mercantile establishment and who has probable cause to believe that a specific person has committed or is committing the retail theft, **may detain the suspect** in a reasonable manner for a reasonable time on or off the premises for all or any of the* *following purposes: to require the suspect to identify himself, to verify such identification, to determine whether such suspect has in his possession unpurchased merchandise taken from the mercantile establishment and, if so, to recover such merchandise, to inform a peace officer, or to institute criminal proceedings against the suspect. Such detention shall not impose civil or criminal liability upon the peace officer, merchant, employee, or agent so detaining.*

See my website (crimefightersusa.com) for a link to the pertinent section of your own state's criminal code. I suggest you print a copy of it to keep in your office, and to include with your apprehension paperwork, for those times when a shoplifter, customer, or new employee calls into question your authority to apprehend.

So you have the authority. Now it's time to make that first stop.

Chapter 5 – Taking Control of the Situation

In the often-unpredictable shoplifter apprehension scenario, how do you exhibit control so that the shoplifter knows you are in charge? What can you do to prove to them that you are the competent authority?

First, you must exhibit confidence. Along with that show of confidence you need to display both your lack of fear of confrontation and your determination not to give up. To take control of a situation successfully, you need a step-by-step process to follow. This process varies slightly for juveniles and adults, as well as for males and females. Some unique situations require a modification of these procedures, yet you still need a standard procedure for the typical cases you will face on a daily basis. Remember, you are making an arrest, which means you are restricting someone else's freedom. Knowing how to approach a suspect, and what to say when you do, are the first two steps in the process of a successful apprehension.

The six basic steps of apprehending a shoplifter are:
- Impede their progress
- Identify yourself
- Return the suspect to the store
- Use minimum force
- Obtain a witness
- Escort them back to the office

Impede their progress

The way you approach the subject and the first words out of your mouth will set the tone for how well the apprehension goes. Imagine you have witnessed the suspect take and conceal merchandise, leave the store, and begin to walk away, possibly toward their vehicle. The first step is to stop their forward movement. Approach the suspect as quickly and quietly as you can and confidently step in front of them. Most people respond by stopping. You now have their attention! To successfully execute this maneuver, you have to approach them quickly and usually from behind so they do not see you coming. Put the element of surprise to work for you. If a shoplifter notices you approaching from the side, their "flight mode" immediately starts to kick in. You don't want that to happen because that's when all kinds of complications can occur. If they start to run and you end up in a chase, not only do the odds of them getting away increase, but the chance of someone getting hurt increases as well. To make a smooth apprehension, you need to be in close physical proximity. When following them out of the store, you need to stay as close as possible without being seen until you make your move.

Identify yourself

At this point, the stage is yours. As they say in show business, "You're on!" You've just stepped in front of the subject. They're nervous! Your adrenaline is going! They're looking at you and you are looking back at them. What do you do next? What do you say? The most important thing at this moment is to identify yourself.

As a plain-clothes store detective, it didn't take me long to figure out the most effective method. I stepped in front of them, looked them in the eye (eye contact is very important in establishing control) and said, "Excuse me sir, I'm with Store Security. I want to talk to you." Or you can shorten it up, and simply say "Store Security. I want to talk to you." This simple phrase gets the message across. Whatever you say, state it clearly and precisely. It has to be simple and quick. If you are a member of management, say something similar: "Excuse me miss. I'm the assistant manager and I want to talk to you." This is not the time to be nice or apologetic. It is the time to be firm and direct.

At the same time I'm telling them who I am, I also hold my badge or ID card in my hand for them to see. Showing your identification is not only an act of professionalism, but demonstrates your authority to stop them. ID is also a visual form of communication to help them understand the situation. If you are a member of management with your name or title badge pinned to your chest, you could point to your ID as you verbally identify yourself. I made a habit of pulling out my ID and having it ready just before I step in front of them. That way I wouldn't have to fumble for it as I'm identifying myself.

They will be focused on completing their theft act by trying to get away with your merchandise so you need to distract them through the use of your voice, your confident presence in front of them and by flashing your ID. Make sure you hold your credentials at eye level for just a second or two. Make sure they can clearly see your ID but don't give them time to read it. Hold it out, and then tuck it away back in your pocket. You need to have both hands free in case they attempt to get past you. Remember you can show your identification to them later in the office if they request it. By stopping the subject in this manner, you will have effectively gotten their focus off what they are doing. That will only add to your advantage.

Let's look at some examples when taking firm control of the situation led to a successful apprehension:
1. A female shoplifter with several pairs of jeans concealed in her shoulder bag left the store. We had a metal railing about three feet high surrounding the sidewalk immediately outside the foyer. After observing the concealment, I followed her outside. As she walked out between one of the openings in the railing, I ran up and jumped over the railing and came down directly in front of her. After I identified myself, the first words out of her mouth were, "Where did you come from?" The element of surprise definitely put her off her guard and won me some precious minutes of shocked compliance.
2. Another female shoplifter placed a nineteen-inch TV in her shopping cart and pushed it out of the store without paying for it. I came up behind her on the sidewalk, identified myself and grabbed hold of the cart. I then had her turn around and push the shopping cart with the TV back into the store. By grabbing hold of the shopping cart and halting the forward momentum, I simultaneously impeded her progress and immediately got her attention.
3. A male shoplifter with air tools from the automotives department concealed in his jacket walked out of the store without intending or attempting to pay for the items. I

followed the subject outside while radioing for backup. I stepped in front of him and identified myself with ID in my right hand, while also grabbing hold of his jacket with my left hand. This prevented him from even thinking of trying to run. Control of the situation was immediate! However, before taking hold of anyone, check with your particular store or company policy for what you are allowed to do.

In all three examples above, the shoplifters returned to the store without incident. Control of the situation was established before the subject could remove their car keys from their pocket or purse. Those are your first two steps when apprehending a shoplifter: (1) impede their progress, quickly and unexpectedly, and (2) identify yourself firmly and formally. Those two steps alone, when done correctly, should establish who is in charge. Remember also that any shoplifter apprehension can potentially turn into a dangerous situation. Be smart, always call for backup, and use common sense.

These first two steps will establish that you are in control of the situation. But these are only the initial steps in making a successful apprehension. The other steps involved in performing this often difficult and sometimes dangerous task are as follows:

Return the suspect to the store

As we proceed to this next step, there is still a good chance that you may have an uncooperative subject. When stopped, shoplifters commonly say, "What's this all about?" or "I didn't take anything." So, to maintain the control you have just established, when they respond with "What's this all about?" go ahead and tell them. Tell them why you stopped them and exactly what you want. Just make sure it is precise and to the point. For example, "I want the two DVDs you placed in your purse" or "I want the two sweatshirts you hid in your shopping bag" should get the message across. In other words, state to the subject **what** the item(s) is and **where** it is on their person. When they realize you know what they stole and where it is hidden or concealed, you convince them of your professional competence… and that they can't talk their way out of the situation.

Next, a counterintuitive tactic: don't let them give you any stolen merchandise unless it's something very small that could easily be lost. Make them carry it all back into the store. They don't even have to remove the item(s) from where they've concealed it. Again, you don't want to have to carry any of it yourself except perhaps the smallest pocketable object. It needs repeating that you must keep your hands free in case they try to run. And trust me, some of them will try to run if you give them the slightest opportunity, right up until the moment you walk them back to the store and sit them down in your office.

While you escort them back into the store, continually talk to them: Ask them their name, how old they are, where they live, whether they are with anyone, whether they are enrolled as a student somewhere. This will distract them so they're not thinking of trying to get away. And if you have multiple shoplifters, your continual chatter keeps them from talking to each other to get their stories straight. This is where your backup comes in handy as you divide the suspects between you to keep them from communicating with each other. Plus, by asking them questions you will establish a rapport so they'll be more cooperative back in your office. Begin your basic questioning as you take them back inside.

Use Minimum Force

When you have confidently stopped someone using the methods I've described, most people won't need any more convincing that you are in charge, and they will come back into the store with you without any problems. Then there's the rest. You may need to place your hand on their arm or shoulder to guide them back into the store as you walk beside them. Remember, at any moment they may try to run away from you. Be prepared to hear sob stories and excuses such as they have never been arrested before, or never been in trouble and it's all a big misunderstanding. More likely they've just never been caught before. So keeping one hand on them prevents their running away, especially juveniles.

For most people a gentle guiding and your professional conduct is enough to get them back into the store. You're not trying to embarrass anyone. You just want to get them to your office as quickly and as quietly as you can. And if you act professionally and politely, most people will follow your directions. But what about someone who will not cooperate? Returning an uncooperative shoplifter takes an entirely different expertise and qualities that are foreign to most people. We are not just confronting someone now but restraining them. In other words, "getting physical," either by using some type of hold to control them, or possibly even handcuffing them in order to bring them back to the store.

The uncooperative shoplifter might be someone with a prior arrest or even a serial professional thief with multiple arrests. Some people just panic when caught. Others are unable to take responsibility for their actions at that moment. Whatever their criminal history or attitude at the time, people who flee do not want to be caught in the commission of a crime. At this point, as they attempt to break away from you, you don't have many options left other than to get physical.

When getting physical, a key point to remember when attempting to apprehend a shoplifter is "the use of minimum force." What is the minimum force necessary for our purpose here? We've all heard stories of police officers using excessive force, an accusation we ourselves naturally want to avoid. Minimum force is simply the least amount of force necessary to make a successful apprehension. Your knowledge and experience, as well as the attitude and determination of the shoplifter, will determine the minimum amount of force necessary in each situation.

Believe me, what you want to avoid is a wrestling match! Once a serious struggle begins, our initial goal is to get them off their feet and down on the ground so they can't run. Once this is done, you and your backup have a better chance of restraining this person.

You can manage a previously uncontrollable person with handcuffs, which is a huge asset when returning an uncooperative shoplifter to the store. You should get authorization to carry restraints from your employer. Carrying and using handcuffs is a big responsibility. You must know how to use them safely and correctly. Get trained and certified and be aware of all local and state laws concerning their use. If you do decide to use handcuffs on a shoplifter, for your safety and theirs, do not remove the handcuffs from them until the police arrive.

At this point you may have some questions: what do you do when they run, how far do you chase them, and what do you do when you finally catch them?

I always give chase! Maybe it is just me, but I always take it as a personal challenge. So if someone shoplifts from my store and tries to get away by running, I'm going to pursue them and catch them. I've always been in good shape and have no qualms about chasing after someone. I didn't catch every person I chased, but I usually recovered the items taken. In the pursuit of any thief, you need to have a reasonable chance of catching the person quickly. Be honest, are you fast enough? What kind of shape are you in? Even more important is the safety issue. Is the chase leading into traffic? Or maybe to someplace where his friends are waiting?

There are other variables to consider. Most importantly, what is your store policy? A good rule of thumb for those who must write their own pursuit policy: once the subject leaves the parking lot area, let the police handle it. Also consider how you will end a chase you can't win! Once a chase begins, you can usually tell within the first few seconds whether you are closing in on them or not. As soon as you realize you probably will not catch them, always yell: "Drop the merchandise!" Amazingly, they usually comply, turning a potential loss into a partial victory.

When you do catch a fleeing suspect, they'll probably need to be restrained. Or held somehow at the location until the police arrive, which they will sometimes arrange themselves, accidentally. A perfect example of this occurred when I was working at the local Wal-Mart and attempting to stop a shoplifter. He fled, and I chased him up a small hillside and into a nearby office building. I paused outside to radio my partner to cover the back of the building. Upon entering the front entrance, I asked the receptionist if she had seen anyone come inside. She said a man had just run in and asked to use the restroom. After she pointed out the restrooms to me, and confirmed there were no other exits from the men's room, I told her we were in pursuit of a suspected shoplifter and asked her to call the local police for me. My partner and I waited outside the men's room until the police got there. There was no need for us to enter as the man was essentially trapped; there was only one way out. Once the police arrived, I informed them of the shoplifting incident and subsequent chase, ending here. The police officers entered the restroom and took the subject into custody. After getting the rest of the details from us, the police escorted him to the store to complete our paperwork before charges were filed.

Nowadays people are lawsuit-happy, so you had better know what you are doing before arresting, restraining, or handcuffing someone for a crime you suspect them of committing. For example, if the suspected shoplifter doesn't want to come back into the store with you and begins to resist, I wouldn't recommend getting into a struggle with someone you might not be able to budge. There are ways to verbally convince the subject to come back into the store with you without backing down. Attempting to restrain the subject should be your last resort.

Here are three examples of things you can say as the subject becomes uncooperative:

- "You can come back into the store and talk to me, or you can talk to the police, it's your choice."
- "If you walk away, I will get your license plate number, call the police, and have them arrest you at home in front of your family and neighbors. Is that what you want?"
- "If you have good ID, no prior arrests, and cooperate 100%, we don't have to involve the police." (This is usual policy for small dollar amounts. In these cases the store has the option of civil demand, which we will discuss in more detail in a later chapter.)

Another option would be to tell them to sit down right there in the parking lot or on the sidewalk and wait for the police (who should have been called before you went out the door). This happened to me only once, when a woman absolutely refused to come back inside and sat right down on the sidewalk. And that is where the cops picked her up!

Whether restraining someone by grabbing hold of their jacket or running after and tackling a suspect who tries to get away, I am often faced with intense situations with shoplifters determined to get away. Most don't succeed. Why would I put myself in these situations? I've always had a strong sense of responsibility, to do my job to the best of my ability. And for me that meant catching the thief, not just recovering the merchandise. Remember if you are unable to apprehend and restrain them, they will be free to cause grief and loss to someone else's business or even return to your store to do so. And as I stated before, I take it as a personal challenge whenever someone comes into my store and tries to get away with theft. The choices you make when faced with a fleeing shoplifter will be determined by your own personal motivation and guided by your employer's written policies.

Obtain a Witness

Either before you leave the store to make the apprehension or immediately upon reentering, you need to get someone, preferably another employee, to be a third-party witness to the process. In a large department store, this should never be a problem with many employees working in different areas. At one store there was a photo center across from our security office with several store associates who were more than willing to sit in as a witness whenever the need arose. Also, you can always go to the customer service desk and call for a member of management to sit in as your witness. Or if you are carrying a radio, just call them to meet you at your office. Actually, anyone available can serve as your witness, from management to a salesclerk. They are not only there to observe, they are also there for your protection.

In a smaller store with few employees on hand, finding someone to be your witness might be difficult, especially if the only other employee is running the cash register. In that case, leave a door open so you are not alone in the office with the suspect behind a closed door. If you have a witness that can sit in with you, feel free to close the door for privacy. Another option is to simply call the police, and don't do anything until they get there.

Why should you bother obtaining a witness?

1. To protect yourself legally. If you apprehend a shoplifter of the opposite sex, proceed with caution! You will need to have a same-sex witness present in that office with you as well. If you are a male and you stop a female shoplifter and return her to the store, I don't care whether she is thirteen, thirty-three, sixty-three or older, if you plan on taking her to a private office anywhere in the store, you better have a witness in there with you. All she has to do is say you promised to let her go or

be lenient in exchange for sexual favors, or that you assaulted her, and you haven't got a leg to stand on. If this happens, guess what? Your career is over. But if you have a witness sitting in on your interview, they can testify as to what was said and what went on during the interview (see #2 below). If you are a female detective and you apprehend a male shoplifter, this goes for you too. If you are ever in doubt, get a witness the same sex as the shoplifter!

2. To be your backup. Your witness, whether it's a cashier, a member of management, or another security associate is your second set of eyes and ears. They may see things you miss because you're busy filling out a report and have your head down. Suppose your witness sees the suspect surreptitiously toss something under the desk and it turns out to be their stash of drugs. Lucky for you, you had an observant witness, otherwise you might not have found the stash for days and how would you explain those illegal drugs to a supervisor? Your witness may also hear the suspect say something incriminating or abusive which you miss at the time. Anything that is said or admitted to by the shoplifter can be corroborated by your witness... as long as you have one.

3. To protect yourself physically. There is strength in numbers. At this interview phase of the apprehension, if you have a second person sitting in with you the suspect will be less likely to get up and walk out, and possibly assault you as they try to escape. The same thing goes for when you stop them outside. If there is more than one of you making the apprehension, the shoplifter will think twice about getting physical or running away. Most women, whether store detectives or management, will feel safer if they have a male witness to sit in on their interview, especially if they have apprehended a male shoplifter.

Escort them back to the office

Earlier we talked about guiding the subject by the arm in order to lead them back into the store. Remember to use the minimum force necessary. A little nudge of their elbow is sometimes all it takes to steer someone back in. And if you have your witness, let them lead the way back to your office. You've got enough to concentrate on as you walk the subject back in.

As you begin escorting your subject, walk beside and a little behind them, never in front of them. You want to be able watch their hands to see that they don't dump any merchandise before you get back to your office. If the stolen item is something small, they might try to get rid of it. So I ask for the tiny goods right after I stop them. You don't want to recover all the merchandise outside because then you have to carry it and it ties up one of your hands. But it's better than losing valuable stock and having someone accuse you of a false arrest.

Continue talking to the subject as you walk them back. They may be asking you a lot of questions at this time such as, "What's going to happen to me?" or "Do you have to call my parents?" or "Why can't you just let me go?" You will have a much more cooperative shoplifter if you are able to ease their fears by answering their questions. Expect them to be nervous and even scared. However, for any noncompliant shoplifter my best answer was always: "Your cooperation will determine what's going to happen from this point forward!"

You now have all the basics for making an apprehension. You've stepped in front of the subject, identified yourself, and returned them to the store. You have recovered any small easily-ditched stolen merchandise. Hopefully they've been cooperative and you haven't had to use any amount of force. You've obtained a witness to sit in on the interview with you, and you are escorting the subject to your office to be processed.

So what happens when you finally do get back to your office? Why are you taking this person there? What should be your intent at this point in the whole apprehension process? What are the first things you should do after opening the door and asking the subject to have a seat?

We will explore the answers to all these questions in the next chapter.

Chapter 6 – Processing the Perpetrator

Congratulations! You confidently followed the suspect outside and made the apprehension. You successfully returned them to the store, obtained a witness, and established that you are in control of the situation. Now you want to maintain that control as you escort the subject back to your office and begin the interview process. As we begin, remember this is not an interrogation but simply an interview. During the interview process, there are three stages we will look at: the pre-interview, processing the subject and juvenile procedures.

Part I: The Pre-Interview

The pre-interview stage will not only confirm to them that you are in charge, but it will show the subject that you are an experienced professional. In the pre-interview stage, the first three things you do are:

- Recover your merchandise
- Obtain identification
- Read them their rights

As you walk the subject back to the office, your heartbeat probably hasn't slowed down yet. Nervous energy is still flowing. You may be breathing heavily if you had to chase this person down. The shoplifter, also out of breath, may have temporarily given up trying to get away, but you can bet his mind is racing as to how he can weasel his way out of this. Don't give him or her a chance to think. Keep the process moving by continuing to engage the person in conversation. Everyone at this point will still be a little hyped up. Ask questions. Keep his or her mind occupied as you walk back to your office. Once you get there, it's time to take a deep breath, calm down, and take care of business. As you enter your office and the interview phase, you begin with the three pre-interview objectives in mind, beginning with recovering your merchandise.

Recover your merchandise

This person took something from your store without paying for it. Your initial objective is to get it back while maintaining control of the situation. The first thing I will say to a subject as we enter the office is, "Have a seat and put my merchandise on the desk." From those first words, most people will take out the item(s) from where they concealed it, and lay it down right where I tell them. They are being compliant and respecting my authority. Notice that I tell them, "Put <u>my</u> merchandise on the desk." It doesn't matter if you're the manager, the assistant or with security. If they steal from your store, they are stealing from you. Calling it "my merchandise" lets them know this is a little more personal to me than just taking something from some big, impersonal company. It also sounds better than saying, "Put the store's merchandise on the desk." Depending on where they concealed it on their person, you can use other initial phrases such as "Okay, dump the purse!" or "Remove the jacket!" or "Empty your pockets!" to get your message across. If you know they only took one particular item, go ahead and be specific, and tell the subject what you want. Remember, your objective is to get your stuff back.

Other ways to recover your merchandise are:

1. Use leverage. At any point in the interview process, if the subject is uncooperative (for example, they refuse to remove the concealed items), you have the option to pick up the phone and call the police. That usually gets their attention. During one interview as I picked up the phone, the subject said to me, "Who are you calling?" I said, "The police, because you won't talk to me." He immediately replied, "You don't have to do that." He then became quite cooperative, even telling me the reasons why he stole from my store.

2. Tell them, "I want everything back." This statement works well when you may have only seen the last item taken, and it's obvious to you that there is more in her shoulder bag than just one unpaid item. Her bag's loaded, and probably with a lot more of your stuff! If you tell the female subject, "I want my

two CD's back that I saw you take," that's exactly what you'll get. She will reach into her shoulder bag and pull out two CDs, just what you asked for. How about, as you enter the office, simply state to the subject, "I want all of my merchandise back, right now, on the desk!" The shoplifter complies of course by dumping the entire contents of her bag/purse, having no idea how much or exactly what you've seen her steal. The key point here is, never let them know how much you know, or how much you've seen them take. You recover a lot more of your merchandise this way. (Note: This is different from when you stopped the subject outside and were being specific as to what was taken, in order to convince them to come back inside with you.) For example, the female subject dumps her purse on your desk, and instead of finding the two CDs that you saw her take, you end up recovering ten. Expect to recover more goods than you may have personally witnessed being stolen.

3. Conduct a search. If they will not surrender the concealed (and now stolen) merchandise, you are within your rights to search the person and anything in their possession, like bags, backpacks, strollers, etc. You can search for two kinds of things: your merchandise, and weapons. If you feel your safety or that of your witness may be at risk, take it upon yourself to conduct a pat-down search of the subject when you first bring them into your office. If you had to chase them or physically restrain them, or if they verbally or physically threatened you, you have good reason for a pat-down search.

The Pat-Down Search: Have them stand up, put their hands on a wall, facing the wall with their feet spread apart. Start your pat-down search under the arms and work your way down to the bottom of their pant-legs. Though searching primarily for a weapon, you may locate additional unpaid-for items on their person. You may also find their identification. Whatever you find, have the subject pull it out and hand it to you. Never put your hand into the subject's jacket, coat, or pants pocket. If you see or feel something in there, have them reach in and pull it out. The last thing you want to do is stick your hand in a pocket and get pricked by a drug user's dirty needle.

The Visual Search: If you don't feel comfortable doing a pat-down search, you can instead do a visual search by having the subject just stand up and turn around. You are obviously looking for bulges in their pockets, waistband or pant-legs. If you see anything out of the ordinary, ask them to show you what's hidden there. Always ask them to empty their pockets.

Remember the witness already present who is the same sex as the shoplifter? Not only are they your protection, but if the occasion comes up where the subject has to be searched or clothing removed in order to return your items, this same witness can stay in the room. You can step out of the office for a few minutes and wait outside until the items are recovered. A member of management makes a good witness since they know the routine and what to look for. This type of concealment is quite common with fitting room thefts where the subject hides merchandise underneath their own clothing and wears it out of the store. Both men and women will attempt this. Guys, if you want to stay employed and lawsuit free, never physically search a female shoplifter. Allow your female witness to do that for you. Ladies, if the male subject has to remove clothing, this goes for you too. If you apprehend a male shoplifter, get a male witness.

Obtain Identification

Your second objective, immediately after recovering your merchandise from the subject, is to find out who they are. Positively identifying the subject will aid in determining your course of action. As a first step, ask for a driver's license or photo identification. If they don't have a photo ID, then anything with a name and address like a recent bill they received in the mail will work.

If they have no ID on their person, a family member or friend can bring their ID from home. I've done this on several occasions. And I've actually used the excuse of identifying someone to make an arrest of a co-conspirator. While covering the electronics department in a Montgomery Ward store, I apprehended a female shoplifter who walked out with hidden merchandise, but not her male accomplice who had concealed the stolen items. They had split up and whenever that occurs you go after the one with the merchandise. When it turned out she didn't have any ID, she told the manager and I where she parked and that her friend would be able to identify her. She had no idea we even knew about her friend. I found the car with the male suspect waiting for her. I walked up to the window, identified myself and explained to him that his female friend had been picked up for shoplifting, and asked him if he could come inside and identify her. He had no idea that I knew he was involved or what was about to take place. Without hesitating he followed me in and verified her name and address. All I had to do was keep him there until the police arrived. To prevent him from leaving, I told him he would need to stick around and verify her ID to the police as well. It didn't take long for the cops to show up. I explained to them what had occurred, and how both subjects had been involved in the theft. Then the officers, without hesitating, arrested them both. The male subject, who thought he was in the clear and, made the mistake of coming back in, was quite surprised. Sometimes, it's all about outsmarting the thieves.

In any criminal matter, no John or Jane Does are allowed. If a subject is not carrying ID, and you have no way of proving who they are, call the police. The police can find out who they are for you. They can also run a background check to see if the person has any prior retail theft convictions. Never release someone you can't identify. If your particular store or company participates in the civil demand program (or something similar in your state), you'll need a true, complete, and current address if you hope to have the subject pay the fine. If you can't find him, you can't make him pay, and the shoplifter escapes scot-free. The police won't release someone until they positively identify them, so why should you? Correct, you're not the police, but without ID you can't prosecute them or use civil demand. We will discuss these prosecution options in detail, in Chapter Nine.

Read the subject their rights

Your third objective is the easiest. All you have to do is read them the Miranda Warning. You may not be required to do so either by your state or the company you work for, but it sure makes an impression on the shoplifter. Do you want to establish your authority with this individual? Do you want them to feel that they are under arrest? Do you want to cover yourself when a defense attorney asks you in court if you advised their client of their rights? Of course you do! Then read them the Miranda Warning. Once you do, you now have their complete attention. And you're covered if and when you go to court.

The following paragraph is a minimal Miranda Warning, as required by the Fourth Amendment to the Constitution:

> *"You have the right to remain silent. Anything you say can and will be used against you in a court of law. You have the right to speak to an attorney, and to have an attorney present during any questioning. If you cannot afford an attorney, one will be provided for you at government expense. Do you understand your rights?"*

I've been to many preliminary hearings and several attorneys asked me this very question right off the bat: "Did you read them their rights?" That's why I recommend doing this as one of the first three things you do upon entering the office.

After you read them their rights, you may choose to continue to talk to or question them. They may decide to exercise their rights and not say anything at all. And that is their right. In that case, you probably won't get a verbal admission. It's also doubtful that they'll sign anything that states admitting guilt or accepting responsibility for their actions. Whether they say or sign anything, or not, it doesn't change a thing legally! You know what you saw this person do and you can testify to it in court.

First, always recover your merchandise. Second, identify the subject. And third, read them their rights. Now you have completed the pre-interview and can settle in to what I call processing the subject, and begin taking care of your paperwork.

Part II: Processing Procedure

There are several key steps to processing a shoplifter:
- Apprehension forms to fill out
- Professional conduct to maintain
- Length of time in the office
- Prosecution policy to observe

Apprehension forms

You've made the apprehension and returned the shoplifter to your office. Next, you've recovered your merchandise, identified the shoplifter and read them their rights. Now, let's finish getting this person processed and out of your office, so you can get back out on the sales floor and catch another one.

You should have a basic apprehension form handy in your office for whenever a shoplifting incident occurs. See the Appendix for a sample blank form you can use. The example I included starts with the Miranda Warning at the top with a place for them to sign indicating they have been read their rights. Next comes your store information, a place for you to enter the subject's personal information, as well as a line for juvenile offenders. At the bottom is a section where you will describe the items taken and the retail dollar value of each. Lastly, you will want to have any witnesses with you to sign their names as well. Feel free to use this sample form and make any modifications you feel necessary.

Professional conduct

Your professionalism, the way you handle yourself and the shoplifters you deal with, will say a lot about you personally and your company. The company's reputation, as well as yours, is on the line every time you decide to stop someone. How do you treat people, especially shoplifters? Unless you've been trying to catch this person for a while, you have no idea what kind of person you've just caught. They could be a dirt-bag, a drug addict, a con-artist, or they may be an upstanding citizen. I've caught the president of a local company, a church secretary, a family member of a TV reporter, and even a state trooper. Being polite and treating people with respect while doing your job can go a long way in developing rapport and obtaining cooperation. When they cooperate, your ability to keep it low-key speaks to people who know they made a stupid mistake. When you make an apprehension, you're not trying to embarrass anyone. They do that to themselves. You are simply doing your job. So do it to the best of your ability!

Length of time in the office

Different companies have differing views on how much time you should spend with someone in your office. Anywhere from 30 to 45 minutes is about the average time required to process a shoplifter. But that's just a target to shoot for. I don't ever remember any of us letting someone go because we ran over an allotted time. So as a rule, you keep them there until the job is done. You may have to wait for a parent to arrive, a family member to bring an ID, or a police officer who is tied up on another call. That kind of delay is a perfect time to educate yourself by talking to the person you've arrested and finding out the real story behind their choice to steal from your store. You'll be surprised at what you can learn about human behavior. You might find out things like why they picked your store and what the street value is for reselling your merchandise.

You might also learn whether they have a drug problem, a relationship breakup problem, or a not-getting-enough-attention-at-home problem. This is all assuming they want to have a conversation with you, of course. Their openness will depend on your personality, whether you're a people person or not, and the mood of the subject. They may just need someone to talk to and you could be that person. You don't have to have any professional counseling skills, just be a good listener. If the subject is a juvenile, you have a chance to make an impression on a young person's life, to steer them in the right direction.

This goes for adults as well. I've had adults break down and cry in my office after telling me what was going on in their life and how sorry they were for what they did. On the other hand, I have also gotten sob stories from many whose sole intention was to get me to feel sorry for them, to let them go. Usually these people have been arrested before. They'll try to play you like they do everyone else. So you'll get both kinds. You've got to be able to discern between the two. But go for it. If you have to wait with someone and have the inclination to chat, and they do too, use it as a learning experience to make you better at what you do.

Prosecution policy

Towards the end of the interview process, review the penalties in your state with the shoplifter. Let them know what they are up against. For example, in the state of Pennsylvania, most people don't know that a third conviction for retail theft is a felony offense! That little-known fact usually gets me a very surprised response.

As far as involving the police, your store or company should have a prosecution policy you are expected to follow. If you don't have one, you need to put one in place. In general there are four options open to you after you've completed your processing of the subject:
- Release them with just a warning
- Ban them from your store
- File criminal charges
- Offer civil demand

Your options will depend on what state you reside and work in, as well as your own store policy. If you are the store owner, take the time to research these options and outline your own policy before you have a shoplifter sitting across from you in your office. These topics will be covered more fully in Chapter Nine.

Part III: Juvenile Procedures

In the previous section, I spoke of a chance to make an impression on a young person's life. Anytime you catch a juvenile shoplifter in your store, you are presented with a potentially tremendous opportunity. You have a chance to speak up and be heard at a time when most adults in their life are being tuned out. You are the person who caught them. You know their secret. You know something about them now that maybe their parents, their teachers, and possibly their friends don't even have a clue about. So, what can you do with it? As mentioned previously in this chapter, take advantage of any time you have to educate the juvenile offender, and let them know they are going down the wrong road!

We define a juvenile as anyone less than eighteen years of age. We're talking about children, someone's kid. Maybe yours? We will discuss three areas regarding juveniles: apprehension, processing, and the parent conference.

Apprehension

You apprehend a juvenile the same way you would an adult. Never forget that you are handling someone's child, though. Treat them the way you would want your kids treated. And once you do apprehend them, you are responsible for them while they are in your custody. You weren't expecting that, were you?

Kids take stupid things, usually the latest hot item from toys or electronics. They'll also go for clothing, cosmetics, food items, and cigarettes if they can get to them. If there is a small group of them, a lot of times the smallest or youngest is prodded to steal something to prove their mettle to their peers. This youngster should also be the easiest to catch because they are the least experienced. Remember this dynamic the next time you have a group of kids stealing and you can only catch one of them.

A lot of kids will run from you. So before you decide to apprehend a juvenile shoplifter in your store, you better be ready for a chase. Most kids who run are scared and don't know what else to do. They'll also run if they have been in trouble before, whether it's retail theft or something else. (That's also why adults run.) If a kid's been caught once before, they've been through the system. They're not stupid; they know what's at stake. They don't want to be caught again. But it is also obvious they didn't learn from their previous experience.

Processing

With adult shoplifters, the first three things you do are recover your merchandise, identify the subject, and read them their rights. The only difference with juvenile shoplifters is that you call their parents instead of reading them their rights. You can read them their rights later, in the presence of their parents, if you feel it's necessary. Even if they are carrying appropriate ID, you will still be making a call to their parents. If you get a defiant teenager who won't tell you who they are, and/or has no ID, treat them the same way you do an uncooperative adult and call the police. The police will establish who they are, and their age, for you. Their parents can pick them up just as easily at the police station or juvenile detention facility as at your store.

There is no need to physically search a juvenile to recover your merchandise. If the kid is being stubborn, wait till the parents get there, and let mom or dad get it for you. Even without my asking, I've had parents conduct their own search just to satisfy their own curiosity. They immediately tell their child to stand up while mom or dad starts going through their pockets. Even if the parents don't do that, once mom or dad tells them to give back what it is they took, it usually comes right out.

Up until the advent of cell phones, I've had kids who were honestly unable to tell me their address or phone number. More common are the ones who gave me a phony address and/or number. But after multiple attempts with several numbers they've given me, I just tell them the only way you are going home is with your parents or the police. That usually invokes a more honest response from them, especially after I tell them they may have to spend the night in the local juvenile center.

If you are going to apprehend a juvenile shoplifter, they should remain in your custody until you release them to a parent, legal guardian or the police. There may be an occasion when you are unable to contact a parent. I've had to call grandparents on several occasions. Siblings over eighteen will do in a pinch. Even a neighbor who knows the family might do. If you can't locate anyone, and the police won't take them, you can always try Children and Youth Services. You may have to play the role of babysitter temporarily if a parent can't be located or is delayed in coming to the store.

In one instance, the parents were out at the movies or shopping and a sibling I spoke to on the phone had to contact them to inform them about what happened. So I had to wait a while for them to show up. Another time when the mom was unable to come to the store, I got her permission to release the kid (on his own) with an agreement they would return together and review what happened.

Parent conference

After you have gone through this enough times, one thing you will see is that mom and dad are probably going to be more upset than their kid you just caught. Occasionally they will be *extremely* upset, and you will need to prepare to handle that.

One example of this was a father who completely lost control. I was sitting at my desk with my back to the door. The boy I had caught was sitting in a chair across from me. We were waiting on the parents, who had been called approximately ten to fifteen minutes earlier. The father arrived at the store, stopped at the service desk to get directions to the security office, and headed back to our location. He found us, came right in, and without warning, walked past my desk and slugged his son. The dad caught me off guard. I never expected a parent to react like that. I was so taken aback by that incident of the father punching his son that I began meeting with the parents *before* they came inside the office. This soon became my trademark procedure anytime I caught a juvenile offender.

My initial goal in meeting with the parents first, before reuniting them with their kid, is to calm everybody down. I want all parties to be on the same wavelength as we enter that office. This meeting can take place anywhere outside your office. Just do it away from the kid. First I'll introduce myself and explain to the parents what happened. Then I'll explain to them what I'm going to do once we enter the office. I'll also ask them if they have any questions and if we are all in agreement as to how I would like to proceed.

After meeting the parents separately, bring them into the office. Make sure you have sufficient chairs in the office for both parents. Once you enter the office you will do the following:
- To begin, if the parents want me to, I may read the juvenile his rights.
- I will explain the retail theft code and the penalties one can possibly face, including expensive fines and possible jail time.
- I'll tell the juvenile offender that he owes his parents an apology.
- I will explain that we have fourteen days to file charges with the local magistrate. If we decide to do so, the juvenile will get a letter in the mail giving the time and place of the court hearing.

The last bullet point is the main point of my talk. Their child is going to be sweating it out now for the next two weeks, checking the mail every day to see if we decided to file charges or to give him a break. This strategy is exactly what I tell mom and dad I am going to do when I meet with them outside before reuniting them with their kid, and parents overwhelmingly agree with this tactic. In most of these cases we don't file charges. You don't have to be overly dramatic and try to put the fear of God into the kid, although the parents may want you to. Going through all of the above in a gravely matter-of-fact way will accomplish most of that for you. This is a crucial time in a child or teenager's life, and may be the first time they've ever faced their parents in a tough situation like this. You have a chance to help them all get through it.

It is possible that if a parent still seems upset, they may threaten physical violence when they get home. I think you have an obligation to the child at this point. Talk to that angry dad: "Sir, can I talk to you outside?" Tell him that you know he is angry, but it would be unwise to take his kid home and take out his anger on him. That will only make the child afraid of the parent, which won't serve any point right now. Rather than fearing his parents, we want the kid to be afraid of entering the system, and what the penal system can do to him or take away from him. Tell the parents that their kid knows he did wrong. He needs to know they still stand by him and love him even when he screws up. And it's obvious he has caring parents or else they wouldn't be here. That's what they need to show their child when they get home. Yes, some sort of punishment is in order—maybe a loss of privileges, something they will now have to give up for a period of time. It may be their cell phone, computer privileges, use of the car, or whatever is fitting. You may have an opportunity to help out the parents as well, by giving them some guidance to get through what can be a painful experience.

When you first make that call to the parents, impress upon them the urgency of coming immediately to the store. Most parents want to know what their child is up to. And most will arrive relatively quickly, since most of the juveniles you'll catch are local kids. I've actually had a few parents that did not care when I called them and told them about their child's theft. But the majority of them do care and will thank you afterwards.

To summarize a key point, never release a juvenile on their own unless you have the parent's consent. I can't emphasize enough the importance of notifying a parent or legal guardian whenever you apprehend a juvenile shoplifter, to protect yourself and the company. If you release that child or teenager without contacting a parent and anything happens to them in the interim, you and/or your company could be held liable.

Having a step-by-step process to handle each shoplifting incident makes your job a heck of a lot easier. But not all of your shoplifting incidents will be by the book. Crooks don't play by the rules. And there are different theft scenarios you are going to run into. We'll look at a few of these scenarios in Chapter 8, but first we need a firm grasp of the concept of "reasonable force."

Chapter 7 – Use of Reasonable Force

Minimum force necessary to effect an arrest

So what is meant by the use of reasonable force? And when is its use valid? We briefly touched on this in Chapter Five, but it is worth exploring the issue more deeply. Just to be clear, we are talking about the minimum amount of force necessary to make an arrest. Whether it's "minimum force" or "reasonable force," in the field of loss prevention, the terms are interchangeable.

To refresh your memory from chapter five, when you have confidently stopped someone in the way I've described, most people won't need any more convincing that you are in charge, and they will come back into the store with you without any problems. Then there's the rest. You may need to guide some of these individuals back in. By this I mean placing your hand on their arm or shoulder to guide them back into the store as you walk beside them. Remember, they may try to run away from you. They may have never been arrested before, or maybe never been in any kind of trouble before. Most likely, though, it's just that they've never been *caught* before. So, keeping one hand on them may prevent their trying to run. This especially goes for juveniles.

Anytime you find yourself in a situation where the shoplifter is resisting your efforts to get them to come back into the store, you will have to either get physical with them or be very verbally persuasive. Probably a bit of both. We have already discussed in chapter four how to talk the shoplifter back into the store. The focus of this discussion is what to do when they can't be talked back in. This is where reasonable force comes into play. It may be simply guiding them by the arm as you walk them back in. But if the shoplifter is actively resisting, "reasonable force" may involve a lot more than that.

So what happens when the arrest doesn't go as planned, when they aggressively resist? In any apprehension situation, you never know what is going to happen. But if you anticipate what the shoplifter may do, you will be ready for anything.

Fight or Flight: Chases

The first thing you should expect after you stop a shoplifter is resistance, either verbal or physical. If you expect every thief to be cooperative just because you step in front of them and identify yourself, you will be quickly disappointed. You may even become disillusioned and frustrated when you find out they're not cooperating. However, if you expect to encounter some sort of resistance, whether an argument or something more, you will be prepared for it. And if you anticipate it, you will be able to take control of the situation much more quickly. Some will try to talk their way out of it. What we are concerned with here are the ones who have only one escape plan—to run!

When someone decides to run, you have three options available to you:

> **First,** you can let them go. If this is your choice, you might as well look the other way, or pretend it didn't happen. Putting it simply, this is the worst thing you can do since it will only encourage them and others to hit your store again and again. You are definitely making a statement here. Unfortunately, it's the wrong statement. The same goes for when you catch someone, and then just let them go with a warning after you recover your merchandise. You haven't solved the problem; you've only prevented one theft. When you release someone without any penalty or requirement for restitution, you have just sent a message not only to this person, but to the criminal element at large that your store won't fight back. Wrong choice! What's next? Are we going to open the door for them as they walk out with our goods? Shall we hold their bag as they stuff it full of our merchandise? "Catch and Release" may work in a fishing tournament, but it does not work here.

> **Second,** you can go after them. This is my preferred option for several reasons. I will get into it later in this chapter.

Third, you can call the cops and let them handle it. This may be the safest route, but it will rarely recover your merchandise. Remember, the police respond after the fact. Unless you are able to obtain the thieves' license plate number or identify them in some other way, the chances of them being caught are slim to none. Plus, the police will rarely respond to a shoplifting incident unless you have already apprehended the subject. They are more likely to just file a report for their records in case it happens again.

Let's go back and talk about the second option: going after the subject. This is my preferred option for several reasons. Mainly, it gets the job done! You take care of the problem from start to finish. You witness the theft, you identify the thief, you catch the thief and you recover your merchandise. But it also gets results for you down the road. Every shoplifter you catch (and punish) prevents future thefts by that same person. The only way to stop a chronic shoplifter is to catch them and put a stop to their criminal activity. Similarly, if you have a mouse running loose in your house, you won't get rid of him by scaring him away. He'll just keep coming back. You have to put out a mousetrap and catch the mouse. When you do, that mouse won't bother you again. That goes for shoplifters, too.

One question you will want to take into account as you make your decision to chase or not to chase: do they still have your merchandise? Unless they were able to pass it off to an accomplice, or you saw them drop it, they still have it. So, let's assume they do have your merchandise, and you decide to chase them. There are a couple of other questions you need to ask yourself:

- If you go after them, can you catch them? Are you physically able to run after someone with the possibility of catching them?
- Is there a reasonable chance of recovering that merchandise with limited risk to yourself or others?
- If they stop running and instead take a swing at you, can you defend yourself?

If you do decide to chase them, what happens if and when you catch up to them? Just because you catch up to them doesn't necessarily mean they are going to give up and surrender to you. It can't be that easy, and it usually isn't. There are so many factors to consider. How many of them are there? How far away from the store are you? Could they have a weapon? Do they have someone waiting for them? A lot of things to think about.

If you catch up with the subject but they continue to run, you will probably have to take them down. By this I mean get them off their feet by any means possible. And even after you accomplish that you may end up wrestling them on the ground and holding them there until the police arrive. I'm not talking about just grabbing a scared kid by the scruff of his neck and pulling him to a stop. Unless you are so much larger than the adult you are chasing that they seem child-sized to you, stopping them and subduing them will be an entirely different matter.

If they have merchandise concealed inside their jacket or clothing, it usually falls out during the altercation. If all you want to do is recover your merchandise, you could let them go at this point. But why would you? You have just apprehended a shoplifter. Now finish your job, and bring them in!

Let's examine a few chases…

Zayre's Department Store, Butler, PA (Top Ten Case #6) – I first observed and recognized the subject as he entered the store. About ten minutes earlier, I had received a call from Montgomery Ward security to be on the lookout for an individual fitting the subject's description. Now that he had been spotted, I had an associate return the call to inform Ward's security that the subject was now in my store. He was carrying a beige colored jacket over his arm as he headed back to the Electronics Department. Once there, he looked at phones and selected a display cordless phone from off the shelf. He then placed it under his jacket and walked out of the department. He proceeded up the middle of the store, then turned right and exited the store without attempting to pay for the item. I followed the subject out the doors and approached him in the parking lot, but before I could identify myself, he saw me coming and started to run. He threw the phone underneath a nearby car and headed for a local park near the store. I made sure I recovered the phone before pursuing the subject. After I retrieved the phone, I ran back to the store and handed it to an associate. Just then, a car squealed into the parking lot with two security officers from Montgomery Ward inside. They slowed down, opened the passenger door, and I jumped in. The subject was now far ahead of us, but we quickly caught up to him as we sped over to the park. We got out, preparing to chase him on foot. He initially attempted to hide in the tall grass, but after realizing he was outnumbered he surrendered to us and returned to the store without incident. He was later charged by Butler Township Police with retail theft and taken into custody.

J.C. Penney, Ross Park Mall (Top Ten Case #4) – I first observed the subject as he was standing in the Athletic Apparel Dept. As I was walking past the greeting card display I saw him look up several times from the rack of sweats he was standing behind. I continued on past him into Furniture, noted the time on my watch, then entered the Receiving area where I ran up the steps and into the booth overlooking Athletic Apparel. I continued to observe the subject from the booth. I could see a scrunched-up piece of black clothing in his right hand, matching the items on the rack directly in front of him. He kept looking around, and then he placed the item into a small grey bag and left the department. I left the booth and came out of the Receiving doors, immediately spotting the subject heading towards the exit doors between Furniture and Lamps. I radioed for backup, followed the subject outside, identified myself as store security, and attempted to stop him. He immediately started to run through the parking lot and I gave chase. As we passed the Kaufmann's entrance he dropped the bag in which he had concealed the merchandise. I stopped to pick up the bag, then continued after him. I also continued to radio for backup, describing our location and heading. At this time my partner arrived on the scene from the left and almost caught up with the subject before he climbed over a fence separating the mall property from the woods.

My partner and another associate pursued the subject while I came back and handed the bag to one of our other detectives. I then started running down Mall Drive when a member of Kaufmann's Security picked me up in his car and took me to the bottom of the hill. We drove around all the office buildings searching for the subject. I then got out of the car and walked up the hill through the woods to Woodland Road above, in an attempt to get in front of the subject. Unfortunately this guy ran like lightning; he outran all our detectives.

After nearly ten minutes, my partner radioed that he had spotted the subject ("I've got an actor"), and that the subject had crossed Woodland Road several blocks back from my location. A Ross Township police cruiser then arrived and I told the officer that the subject had been sighted. I jumped into the back of the cruiser and we spent twenty minutes searching the neighborhood, unable to find him. At that moment the subject was again spotted by the other security associate, this time heading towards McKnight Road. Via radio, this associate kept me informed of the subject's location and heading while I relayed the information to the officers. We came down Seibert Road and turned west onto McKnight Road when the other security associate radioed that the subject was running down the middle of McKnight Road. Within seconds we spotted the subject, with a Pennsylvania state constable chasing him on foot down the middle of the six lane highway. The Ross Township officer used the police cruiser to cut off the subject, which also blocked the westbound lanes of McKnight Road. The subject stopped only when he ran into the cruiser and was immediately placed under arrest and handcuffed by the Ross Township officers right in the center of McKnight Road. He was returned to the Loss Prevention office after a brief search for his car, a blue Ford. While in the police cruiser, the subject kept saying that some guy was going to kill him if he didn't get him a pair of sweat pants. He also seemed more concerned about the damage to his black leather jacket, which had gotten scratched up in the chase, than with his part in this whole incident. He wasn't making a lot of sense.

He picked the wrong day to come into the store, since we had a full staff working that day. Security and police filled out the proper paperwork, and the subject was photographed by Mall Security and later released, after being issued a citation, since he had ID and no priors.

Joseph Horne's Store, South Hills Village Mall – While walking past the Young Men's Department, I saw the subject and a friend of his enter the department from the mall entrance. After conversing, both left into the mall and I heard the friend say to the subject, "Get me a size 38." The subject came back into the store and after several minutes selected one pair of dark green jeans from the display rack near the entrance. He removed the hanger, and then walked out into the mall with the jeans. As I approached the subject, he saw me coming behind him and started to run. I gave chase and caught up to him rather quickly, grabbing him from behind resulting in both of us falling to the floor. He was cooperative and offered no resistance from this point forward.

Be familiar with your company or store policy and be aware of the potential risks of any given situation. If you are not permitted to give chase, or if the situation appears dangerous, then the answer is obvious. You don't chase! There is nothing wrong with being cautious. No amount of merchandise is worth risking injury, your life, or someone else's. But that doesn't mean you just let them all go. That's option #1, remember?

The point is to stop future thefts from occurring. <u>Every time you have someone arrested, all future thefts by that person have been eliminated or at the very least severely hindered</u>. Your willingness to fight back will send a message to others as well: that they, the shoplifters, the thieves, the con-artists, should think twice before coming into your store. So even though you've recovered your merchandise you should bring them back in, process them (as outlined in the previous chapter), and then call the cops.

Recoveries

There is more than one way to recover your merchandise. We've just talked about what happens when you get involved in a chase, and what it sometimes takes to successfully apprehend a suspect. What's interesting is that most thieves never expect to get chased. They assume that if they are careful enough, everything is going to go their way. There is a false sense of confidence or arrogance that they will complete the theft, leave the store without anyone noticing, and go home to enjoy the fruits of the crime. And up until now, if they've never been caught before, that's exactly what has happened. But when it doesn't go their way, and someone is actually chasing them, they are scared to the point where all they care about is getting away. And if they are scared because someone is chasing them, this can work in your favor.

How it works in your favor is simple. In these situations what usually happens when you approach a shoplifter outside is that they see you before you can identify yourself, they run, and you immediately give chase. When you are within earshot, and before they get very far, you yell as loudly and forcefully as you can: "Drop the merchandise!" (First mentioned in Taking Control of the Situation, Chapter 6). I am convinced this has to be, by far, the most successful phrase in the history of loss prevention. I am still surprised by how many thieves will just throw down their item right there on the pavement, almost immediately after hearing those words as they continue to run. It won't work on all of them, but the use of "verbal force" may sometimes work for you, which means you don't always have to use reasonable force to recover your items.

Defending Yourself

If a shoplifter starts swinging at you or initiates any physical violence, you obviously have a right to defend yourself. My personal philosophy was to do what I had to do to take them down, then hold on until my backup or the police arrived. Whether it was to swing back at them, use a wrestling hold, or just tackle them and hold on for dear life, I did whatever I could do to slow them down so they couldn't get away.

That's exactly what happened one Fall day outside a Zayre's store in Baden, PA. The subject and a female companion walked out of the store with stolen merchandise. When I attempted to stop the young man, he immediately resisted and started swinging. My reaction was to swing right back, and I landed a few punches. He was about my size, maybe a little shorter. As I swung back I realized a quick way to end this. I simply ducked down and grabbed him around his legs. I lifted him up and put him on his back onto the pavement, effectively knocking the wind out of him. That was the end of the fight. Soon my detective partner showed up and we took the suspect into custody. I used that same tactic on several other apprehensions that escalated into a confrontation. Each time I was able to get them off their feet and hold on until the cops or my back-up arrived.

Strength in Numbers and Calling for Back-up

"Back-up!" There's no better news a security officer can hear than a police officer or another associate arriving to back him up. Whenever you are in a tough situation, you want to know that someone will be coming to assist you. And in any shoplifter apprehension, you never know if it's going to get crazy. I discovered that the old adage about strength in numbers is true. On many occasions I've had a shoplifter much bigger than me give up and just come back in quietly, only because there were two or more of us making the apprehension instead of just one.

Most of the time, I worked in large department stores with plenty of associates around. I always made it a habit to see who was available whenever I was about to make an apprehension. There's always someone stocking shelves or moving freight onto the floor. And most of the young guys are more than ready to help out when you have to stop someone. They're eager and full of testosterone, and that can be a huge plus when you are taking on someone larger than yourself. Just remind anyone who assists that you are in charge, and have them follow your instructions to the letter.

Your best bet is to have a member of management follow you out. But how do you notify a member of management, a salesclerk, or anyone else, that you are in need of assistance? There are several different ways, and we used them all. One way was the creation of a specific security code to use over the public address system. The code simply meant security was in need of assistance. I would only use it when I was not able to find another person in time to accompany me. As I was going past the customer service desk, I would tell the person working there to do a "Code 13." They in turn would announce it over the PA system. Whether it was "Code 13" or "Code 99 - Front for carts," it worked. Usually within a minute I would have every available male stock clerk or salesperson (who was not with a customer) on the front sidewalk looking for me and eager to help. Most of the time I would already be walking the suspect back in, but it was still good to know I had backup if I needed it. We also varied the codes because it didn't take long for the customers to figure out what was going on. After hearing the codes being announced and witnessing some of the incidents on the front sidewalk and in the parking lot, some of the customers knew what was happening and would start showing up outside after hearing our code, to check out the action. To avoid attracting an audience we had to change the codes periodically, so the public wouldn't become too familiar with them.

Another means of staying in contact with fellow employees is the use of two-way radios. They are inexpensive, inconspicuous, and durable. They are small enough to fit in a pocket, or on your belt, and are very simple to use. It's the best tool I ever carried with me. Having radios ensures that you can instantly call for backup, or at least let someone know where you are, and be heard (and replied to) immediately. Eventually, all members of our management team and security were equipped with radios. You learn not to go anywhere without it. As long as you have your radio, you are never alone.

If you have a small shop or are working alone, it will be a little more difficult for you. You may have to exercise more customer service than normal whenever you have a suspicious person in your store. Just your continuous presence close to a potential shoplifter may scare them away. Your best tool will be your cell phone. So, to be on the safe side, right before attempting to stop someone who has just shoplifted in your store, call the police first. Have their number listed as one of your favorites on your cell. Tell them you are about to make an arrest and that you are requesting backup. And finally, stay in touch with nearby shop-owners and alert each other anytime a would-be thief enters one of your stores. For these informal methods of back-up to work best, you need to build a certain degree of community and camaraderie with the businesses, commercial tenants, and law enforcement in your store's immediate neighborhood. Be ready to offer help as much as you ask for it, of course. Find out whether there is a neighborhood watch, a community council, a law-enforcement liaison, a chamber of commerce security committee, or something similar which you can join so that you don't need to reinvent the wheel in this area… but if none of those exist, the watch commander of your local police precinct will probably be delighted to hear that you are interested in helping him start one. These are just some of the creative things you can do to protect your merchandise whenever it's just you guarding the store.

If unsure, unwilling, or just not confident: walk away!

I am not and will never be a big advocate of the Don't Stop or Don't Touch policies. If the company you work for has adopted this policy, they won't be in business for long. However, there may come a time when the smartest thing you can do is walk away. You do want the option to back off, if and when the situation appears unsafe for any reason. And there are a number of valid reasons, such as:

- The subject appears to have a weapon.
- There is more than one subject.
- The subject gets to his vehicle before you can apprehend him.
- Instead of running, the subject turns and tries to pick a fight.

Are you worried about stopping someone? If so, walk away! Stopping someone and accusing them of committing a crime can be very intimidating to someone who is not normally confrontational. Not only is it a little frightening, but you want to be absolutely certain that you are not falsely accusing someone. And that's normal. It's okay to be a little afraid and cautious, because that will make you more aware of your surroundings.

Are you mentally and emotionally able to confront someone who has done something wrong? If not, walk away! Do you have it in you to call a thief a thief? That is what it is going to take to be able to do this job, and to do it with any success. Believing I wasn't confrontational enough kept me from becoming a police officer. But as I soon learned, this job is all about confronting people. And when you become familiar with what it takes, and you develop your own style, it will become second nature to you. You will actually come to enjoy the challenge.

Of course it's possible that you have no intention of sticking your neck out to protect your store's merchandise. You may simply be unwilling to get involved, or unwilling to take a risk for whatever reason. You may not want to stop someone, but please do something. Get a careful description of the thief, their car, write down the license plate number, and report it all to the police.

You cannot allow shoplifters to intimidate you or your staff. You have to be able to stand up to them or to anyone who tries to take something from you, whether it's your merchandise, your dignity, your values, or your freedom. If you follow the training in this manual, you will gain the confidence needed not only to perform this type of work, but also to stand up to other acts of injustice you may come across in life.

Use of Handcuffs

The use of handcuffs on a suspect is serious business. Not only are you making an arrest, but you are taking someone into custody. Everyone who has seen a cop show on television has seen numerous criminals arrested and handcuffed. But the police do it as part of the normal arrest procedure. It's out of their routine when they *don't* handcuff someone. As a security officer or member of management, you are not the police, so you don't handcuff all suspects, just the ones that are out of control. This may be your only means of controlling someone who is uncooperative, unreasonable, or combative.

The first thing you need to have before using handcuffs on someone is the authorization to do so. This can come through your employer, or through local law enforcement, which can train you on how to use them. You want to make sure you are doing this correctly, so as not to injure the suspect, and to ensure your safety and the safety of others. You cuff them when they are unruly or when they pose a danger to you and other people.

First, of course, you have to catch this person or, if they are resisting, get them off their feet. If you can get the handcuffs on a suspect who is resisting, you will have fewer worries when you return the suspect to the store. You now have control of the suspect and the situation. However, they can still move around and do some damage. This is exactly what happened with one suspect at the Horne's store in Natrona Heights, PA.

After observing the female suspect (whom we had failed to catch on several previous occasions) select and conceal children's clothing items in her purse, I approached her as she was nearing the exit doors. I stopped her, identified myself, and attempted to return her to the security office. But she had no intention of allowing me to arrest her. She immediately became belligerent and resisted my efforts to guide her arm and lead her to the office. For her safety and mine I had no choice but to handcuff her right there in the store. The subject still managed to kick over several single-stand displays as I escorted her back to the office. Remember, only her arms were handcuffed behind her back, her legs were not!

Another incident occurred at this same Horne's store, with a male shoplifter I had to wrestle down. After I had observed him conceal multiple clothing items into a shopping bag, he headed for the exit doors. I immediately exited the security perch, radioed for backup and caught up to the subject outside in the parking lot. I identified myself and asked him to return to the store. He replied, "What for?" and handed me two receipts that, after a quick examination, did not match the merchandise he had in his possession. I again asked him to return to the store. His answer was, "I don't think so," and he began to walk away from me without the bag. I then told him he was under arrest and that if he wouldn't come back in with me, I'd have to handcuff him. He repeated the phrase, "I don't think so," and continued walking away. I immediately grabbed him around his legs and wrestled him to the ground. The subject and I scuffled for about a minute until he finally said he would come back into the store if I would let go of him. Because of his size I was unable to get the cuffs on him, so I agreed to allow him to walk back in on his own. He knew he couldn't get away because I was too determined, so he gave up. By now my backup had arrived, and after retrieving the bag of stolen merchandise, we escorted him back into the store.

A third incident was at a Zayre's Department store, and involved a battery thief. The subject, a six-foot-tall, two-hundred-pound male, was observed concealing several packages of batteries inside his jacket. He left the store without attempting or intending to pay for the concealed merchandise. Once outside I approached the subject just as he stepped off the sidewalk. It was snowing and the parking lot was slippery. As soon as I identified myself, the subject began to run. However, he didn't get very far as he slipped on the ice and fell flat on his back. He was momentarily stunned as he laid there. I immediately ran over to him, and told him to roll over and put his hands behind his back. He complied without a word. After handcuffing the subject, I helped him to his feet and escorted him back into the store. He was too shaken to resist. He was big enough, and would have been a problem if he had resisted.

There is another option besides handcuffs that you can use to control someone. By grabbing the back of the suspect's belt or waistline, and with a little bit of leverage, you can control their movements. This time the Horne's store at the Monroeville Mall provided the location. The subject was seen concealing several expensive women's pocketbooks inside his coat. I followed him outside, identified myself, and an altercation immediately ensued. I was able to wrestle the subject to the ground but could not get the better of him until my female partner was able to grab the waistline of his pants from behind. With the subject now under our control, I was able to hold onto him until the police arrived.

There's nothing more satisfying in the fight against shoplifting than watching the police taking an apprehended shoplifter, in handcuffs, out of your store and into a waiting patrol car in full view of associates and customers alike. Not only do you feel like you've done your job, but the public sees the effort your store is putting forth, along with the local police, to tackle the shoplifting problem.

Chapter 8 – Shoplifter Variations

There are many different ways that shoplifting can occur. They are as varied as the thieves you will encounter. Some of these encounters will include accomplices. Generally, an accomplice is anyone who is assisting the shoplifter(s) in any way. They can be as involved as actually participating in the theft, or they can be involved in some other manner such as blocking, handing off a bag, acting as a decoy, or creating a diversion. Someone acting as a lookout would also fit into this category. You will need to keep an eye out for accomplices anytime you identify a shoplifter you suspect isn't working alone.

Roles Accomplices Play:

a) Blocker – This accomplice attempts to prevent you, as security or a member of management, from seeing the theft act. By using their body to block your vision, they are shielding their partner in crime from your eyes or from the camera. They may never physically handle the merchandise, but they are definitely assisting in the stealing of it. They will work side by side with the shoplifter, so they are usually pretty obvious. A professional shoplifter will also use other customers as a shield to hide what they are doing, without the customers even knowing.

b) Bag Lady – A person who provides the means to conceal is also an accomplice in the theft act. They involve themselves by handing a shopping bag, empty purse, or other container to the shoplifter so they can conceal store merchandise inside of it. They might simply pull an empty bag from a jacket pocket or their purse, and give it to their partner. They may or may not physically handle and conceal the merchandise. Of course, they do further involve themselves if they choose to carry the concealed merchandise out of the store.

c) Decoy – Decoys also work as a team along with the shoplifter. They will come into your store ahead of the real shoplifter and appear to be an obvious thief, in order to draw your attention away from the actual theft that is taking place in your store. They may load up a shopping cart with high-end merchandise to get you to follow them. They may pretend to conceal merchandise or actually stash it somewhere in the store. Their entire intent is to tie you up with them, so that the real thief gets away with your stuff. When a shoplifter appears too obvious, they are either inexperienced or a decoy. You'll have to recognize which, and respond accordingly. If they are acting as a decoy, you will need someone to keep an eye on them while you look for the real thief.

d) Diversion – A person who creates a diversion is similar to a decoy. They are not the thief, but they try to pull your attention away from what is really going on. They may fake an accident by falling, and thereby tie you up with frivolous paperwork, writing out a phony accident report. They may knock a display over and even help to pick up the items while their accomplice is stealing from you in another part of the store. They may pull a fire alarm or push open an emergency exit door to draw your attention there. Shoplifters whose accomplices create diversions are difficult to catch or prepare for because you never see it coming, and they are usually gone by the time you realize what is actually happening.

e) Lookout – Lookouts usually concentrate on just one thing. Their task is to locate you and keep an eye on you at all times. They will inform the shoplifter(s) if you or anyone else appears to be getting too close. Now *you* are the person being followed. It is very difficult to observe a shoplifter from the sales floor and know where the lookout is at the same time. One way to defeat a lookout is to remove yourself from the sales floor and watch the subjects from a security window or your camera system.

Lookouts will rarely handle the merchandise, and they will continue to watch out for their partner until that person is safely out of the store.

Apprehending an Accomplice

In order for you to apprehend and arrest an accomplice to a shoplifting incident, two things must have occurred:

1) This person must have been involved in the theft act
2) This person must have *had control of the merchandise*

At any point in the theft act, if the person assisting the shoplifter handles the merchandise in any way, such as physically selecting the items to be concealed, or holding the bag while the other person conceals the items in it, or carries the bag containing the stolen items for any length of time, or pushes a shopping cart out the door with the items inside (either concealed or in plain view), then by his actions he has had control of the merchandise with the intent of stealing it. Now that you can prove control and intent, you can apprehend the accomplice as well as the shoplifter. Without these two factors, you probably have no case against the accomplice. One without the other may not be enough. Let's look at a few examples.

Accomplice Example # 1: I first saw the subject as he entered the store on the lower level. He walked into the Bedding Department and crouched down behind a shelf unit next to a female who was already standing there. I got behind another display unit and from there I was able to observe both subjects. She would hand him the shopping bag she was holding, while he selected sheet sets from the display and placed them into the bag. Every time someone would walk by, he would hand the bag back to her, so she had control of the merchandise as well. After the male subject placed a total of four sheet sets into the bag, the subjects left the department, and headed for the exit doors. In this incident, the male subject committed the concealing of merchandise by placing the items into the shopping bag. The female subject not only handed the bag to her male accomplice (Bag Lady), but she then carried the bag containing the stolen items out of the store. Both subjects could now be apprehended, because both were involved in the theft act, and both had control of the merchandise.

Accomplice Example # 2: While a husband and wife are shopping in your store, the wife selects four packs of gum and places them into their shopping cart which already contains other merchandise. As they continue shopping, the husband picks up two of the packs of gum from the cart and places them in his pocket. The wife happens to be in the next aisle and is not aware of the concealment. When they get to the checkout, only two packs are rung up and paid for. The wife doesn't even notice. Both leave the store with the husband in possession of the two unpaid-for items. Both had control of the merchandise. But in this hypothetical example, the only person you can apprehend is the husband. Even though the wife selected and handled the items, you cannot apprehend her since you cannot prove she was involved in the theft act, especially since she was in a different aisle when the concealment occurred.

By handling the merchandise *and* intentionally participating in the theft act, the accomplice becomes a second shoplifter that you can now apprehend. For every accomplice you can't apprehend, make a note of what they look like and the role(s) they played. When you see them again, you'll know to keep an eye on them, to see if they reprise their role or try something new. They may just be an accomplice this time, but they could be the shoplifter you can apprehend the next time.

The Ticket Switcher

One variation on shoplifting that occurs far too often is ticket switching. This is when the subject removes a price tag from one item and replaces it with the price tag of another item of lesser value. Or, they simply cover up the original price tag with one that has the price they want to pay. Their obvious intent is to purchase the item at a reduced price. They may also be intending to return the item and receive the full price, instead of the reduced price they paid. If they do the switch cleanly enough, keeping the price sticker intact, the cashier will probably never notice. In retail terminology, what they've done is create their own unauthorized markdown. Unless it is a large dollar discrepancy, ticket switcher situations are best resolved at the cash register as they try to pay for the item.

Here is what has worked for me: After witnessing a person switching price tags, it was obvious that they would eventually head for the checkouts. I was able to just wait for them there. As a member of security, I would borrow a smock or name badge from a sales associate, and then get into position beside the cashier and act as a bagger. The cashiers knew that if I got beside them at the checkout, they probably had a ticket switcher in line. We had gone over this very same situation in cashier training. I simply waited for the customer to place the item in question on the checkout counter or belt. Before the cashier could ring up the item, I would pick it up first and inform the customer that I worked in that department. I would tell the customer that the item was priced incorrectly, and would ask if they still wanted it at the correct retail price. Once I stated the price, they always said, "I don't want it then." They would leave without purchasing the item, and the loss was prevented.

When you use this method, the suspect will know their little theft attempt didn't work. It doesn't mean they won't try again. But you have now identified this person and you'll be ready for this ticket switcher if they return and try it again. These types of theft attempts are best handled in-store, and no apprehension is necessary. If you take a case like this to court and the suspect decides to fight you on it, you might have a tough time proving that all of your merchandise is always priced correctly. The only exception is the "large dollar discrepancy" I mentioned earlier: If the ticket switch is over a certain dollar amount (as determined by your store) from the legitimate price for that merchandise, you will have a better chance of winning in court, and you can apprehend and prosecute them, especially if they switch the entire container or box the item comes in. You will have to allow the theft to occur of course, and not stop it at the cash register. It may then fall into the next category of thievery called Theft by Deception.

Theft by Deception

This is a variation of shoplifting that has its own section in the Pennsylvania Crimes Code, Section 3922: "A person is guilty of theft if he intentionally obtains or withholds property of another by deception." Let's look at an actual case I refer to as The Salt & Pepper Bandit:

The subject entered the store and proceeded straight back to the Hardware Department, toward the aisle where painting supplies were kept. I recognized him as soon as he entered the store. He was someone we had been watching and trying to catch for a long time. We called him the "Salt & Pepper Bandit" because of his distinct hair color.

Once in the paint aisle, he selected a boxed paint sprayer, pulled it off the shelf, opened the box, and removed a part from the box. He placed the part on the shelf, closed the box, put it under his arm, and headed toward the front of the store. The subject went right to the customer service desk with the paint sprayer. He explained to the sales associate that he had purchased the paint sprayer previously, but it was missing a key part, and now he wanted to return it and get his money back. In this way, he would steal *only the retail value of the merchandise*, not the merchandise itself: he avoids the difficulty of concealing the merchandise, of trying to get it out of the store unnoticed, and even avoids the trouble of fencing it later, when he would receive much less than its full retail value.

We knew ahead of time what he was going to do, because he had gotten away with it before. Normally a customer can't obtain a refund without a valid receipt unless they strongly argue their case. A quick call from me to the manager recommended that we approve this guy's refund without a receipt, so that we could then apprehend him. We had him right where we wanted him, so the manager called the service desk to make sure the refund was approved.

Per our instructions, the sales associate approved the refund. Once the subject accepted the cash in his hand (a credit slip or gift card would have served equally well), he had completed the theft. As soon as he walked away from the customer service desk and before he could reach the front doors, the store manager and I immediately apprehended him. After local police were called and a background check was made, the subject was arrested and taken into custody. Previous arrests included various retail thefts and even impersonating a law enforcement officer. This was one career criminal who never came back to bother our store again.

In this type of crime, you do not have to allow the subject to leave the store. He has no unpaid-for store merchandise on him. The crime has been committed once he accepts the cash. That's when you have to react and make the stop.

Grab & Run Thefts

Most "Grab and Run" thefts occur with items displayed too close to an entrance or exit door. This is not the place you want to display your most expensive or high-theft merchandise. Remember the "Food on a Plate Principle" I described in Chapter 1. What could they grab and run out the door with? It need not be something small and light enough to run a hundred yards with it clutched in the hand. It could be a big-screen TV or a relatively heavy air conditioning unit (very popular in the summertime). Or how about an entire rack of women's jackets or jeans that just came off the truck and was just put out for display? Bottom line, it can be anything thieves feel they have the opportunity and capacity to get away with in a short amount of time.

In most cases, after the subject is in the store for a few minutes, a getaway car will pull up to the sidewalk directly in front of the entrance or exit. The passenger-side door will open while the engine is running. When the subject inside the store sees the car pull up out front, this is the signal for them to make their move. These types of thefts almost always involve accomplices who will either hold open the entrance doors for the subject or be driving the getaway vehicle.

As mentioned before, big-ticket items such as TVs and air conditioners will most likely go out the door in a shopping cart. Other items such as coats and men's or women's apparel will go out the door over someone's arm, usually about 12 to 18 items, all still on hangers. Once the items are in hand and the getaway vehicle is in place, the suspect will literally run out the door before any associate can stop them. To successfully apprehend them, you have to get to them before they get to the waiting vehicle. You'll have to act fast; all they have to do is jump in and go.

Walkouts are related to these types of thefts, but don't usually involve another person or getaway vehicle. Still, the same kinds of merchandise will appeal to the Walkout thief and the Grab & Run thief, and the item is almost always in plain view. The theft can be as simple as someone picking up a jacket from a rack, putting it over their arm, and walking, not running, out the door.

Ways to combat and prevent Walkouts and Grab & Run thefts:

- Alternate the direction of the hangers for any clothing items displayed near store entrances.
- Use cable coat locks for all expensive outerwear displayed, whether by an entrance or not.
- Use empty boxes of big-ticket items to build your display. And except for one functioning display model, keep the rest in the back.
- Use security signage and cameras at all entrances and exits. Have a standard procedure for copying video clips of Grab & Run thefts (and plain Walkout thefts), for later review by management and law enforcement, and for future employee training.
- Do item counts throughout the day to verify that your displayed inventory is not wandering off.

Smash & Grab Thefts

Smash & Grab thefts are crimes of violence and intimidation. These types of thefts can occur whenever a store has glass display cases to showcase jewelry, perfume, brand name watches, and many other types of small, expensive items. The subjects usually work as a team, and you can be sure they've staked out the store ahead of time. For them, the store was chosen for two reasons: it has the merchandise they want, and they feel it's an easy store to hit.

The subjects will enter the store and position themselves around the display cases. It really doesn't matter where the sales associate is because once the smashing of glass begins, no salesperson would want to be nearby. The subjects will come equipped with tools that are initially concealed. Hammers and crowbars are usually the tools of choice. Once they pull them out, stand back! The glass will break easily. Even safety glass, which doesn't shatter, can still be pulled out of the way after being slammed with a hammer. And the glass presents no problem for our would-be thieves, as they will be wearing gloves to protect their hands. This way they won't leave any fingerprints, either. They may grab individual items such as rings or watches. More than likely, they will grab entire display pads that hold multiple items. They'll have bags to stuff these into, or they'll just jam them inside their jacket or coat. Once each has taken a few items, they will leave in a hurry. There most assuredly will be a getaway vehicle waiting for them outside.

These are serious criminals, and are not your typical shoplifters. First of all, they are carrying weapons, so stay clear! Most of them will have a criminal record with multiple offenses. This means they are also experienced. About all you can do is to have someone follow them to identify the getaway vehicle or perhaps get a license plate number. With this type of criminal activity, that is the most you want to do. This type of crime most closely resembles an armed robbery. If you interfere directly, that's what it could become. These people are dangerous. Don't try to be a hero here.

Ways to prevent Smash & Grab thefts:

- Use visible cameras around the entire counter area. This not only acts as a deterrent, but in case of an actual theft, the cameras may provide images that can be used to identify the culprits.
- Except for a minimal number of functioning samples for display, keep the most expensive items locked in a safe, and make sure the door to the safe is shut at all times. Use dummy display samples of your most expensive items whenever possible.

Flash Mob Thefts – A Recent Phenomenon?

Be on the lookout for a "flash mob" coming to a neighborhood near you. Flash mobs are not necessarily a recent phenomenon. Large groups coming into a store to steal have always been a problem. But when it is organized, driven, and assisted by smartphone technology, this type of theft becomes a new and potent threat. It is usually a group of young people, brought together through social media, coordinating their actions via cell phones, and often organized by a single leader who directs their movements. They will come into a store intent on stealing as much merchandise as they can, without any fear of being caught due to their large numbers. In general, young people may be a little bolder; and when gathered in a group, there is a definite sense of strength in numbers. You could almost call it a type of fearlessness. And when there is no sense of fear or responsibility, people can get hurt. Trying to defend your store against a group of people like this can be dangerous. Here are a few examples of flash-mob thefts:

1) In April 2011, nineteen teenagers entered a G-Star store in Washington D.C. and suddenly made off with approximately $20,000 in stolen merchandise. The employees were overwhelmed and unable to stop this mob of young people.

2) In Chicago, on North Michigan Avenue, also known as the Magnificent Mile, shoplifting arrests of juveniles had already been on the increase. At one store, teens entered screaming and yelling, knocking over displays and stealing clothes worth close to $3,000.

3) In Maryland, between twenty-five and thirty teens walked into a Germantown 7-Eleven store at 1:00 in the morning and proceeded to rob the store of multiple items from shelves and coolers. The entire assault lasted less than a minute.

4) In Dallas, TX, what was described as "a swarm of teenagers" poured into an Exxon Tiger Mart and proceeded to rip off the store and seriously injure the store clerk. Police investigated the incident as an aggravated robbery assault.

5) In Silver Spring, MD, approximately seventy teenagers and young people simultaneously entered and shoplifted from

a 7-Eleven store on a Saturday night. By the time police arrived there were only small groups of people gathered in nearby parking lots. When questioned by police, several had items from the 7-Eleven on them, but no receipts. Eventually about twenty people were identified and those who stole were charged.

Ways to combat flash mobs:

- Help to get the laws changed in your state, to classify flash-mob theft as a robbery instead of petty theft (shoplifting). Hopefully a would-be participant will think twice before taking the chance of being charged with robbery or grand larceny, as opposed to the less serious offense of shoplifting.

- Until the laws change, try to change the way that flash-mob theft is prosecuted. One way to do this when you file charges is to specify that you are holding responsible each individual participant in a flash-mob theft, severally and jointly, for the entire retail loss in that theft. Since the group acted together to commit the crime, each member can be held criminally liable for the total loss and damages involved. The high dollar value of the total is likely to qualify as grand larceny, whereas each person's separate share is more likely to remain petty larceny.

- Have camera systems operating at all times and have signage that alerts customers and potential thieves that their actions are being recorded.

- Focus on apprehending just one of them. In a large group, there is usually one person that can be caught, either the smallest, youngest, or slowest one. It may also be someone who makes a mistake, perhaps by trying to take more than they can carry, or by stumbling and falling in the rush, or someone that is momentarily blocked by their fellows and can't slip out fast enough to escape you. That's the one you go after, the one you can most easily apprehend.

- If juvenile flash-mob theft becomes a recurring problem, limit the number of juveniles that can enter your store at any one time.

Even if you only apprehend one of the flash-mob participants, you now have an individual to identify, process, and prosecute. Part of the mystique and effectiveness of flash mobs is the anonymity of each participant: when one participant is identified and faces prosecution, all sorts of things might happen that may lead to identifying and prosecuting other participants of the flash mob theft, including its instigator, especially if you charge the individual you caught with the damages the whole group incurred. You can do this in a civil suit if the laws of your state prevent you from doing this in criminal court. Either way, the attractive anonymity of the group is shattered, and word will get around quickly that your store is not a cool and fun place for a flash mob.

Organized Retail Crime

Organized crime has been with us since the turn of the last century. It's been involved in everything from alcohol, illegal drugs, loan sharking and prostitution. Now it's sinking its claws into retail theft. The FBI estimates losses attributed to Organized Retail Crime (ORC) may reach as much as $30 billion a year. In almost all cases, the thefts involve high dollar amounts, usually in the thousands. This is shoplifting at the highest level; professional thieves at their best. And they will use everything we have talked about previously, from getaway vehicles, to lookouts, to working in teams. How does a retailer, especially a small business owner, combat organized crime when it goes after his merchandise? And where does this stolen merchandise go? It's not all ending up in flea markets. Sometimes it finds its way back to the very store from which it was stolen.

According to the FBI, the stores targeted for theft run the gamut from your local grocery chain to Wal-Mart to boutique shops found at your local mall. In fact, retailers can be their own worst enemy. Once the merchandise is passed down the chain to crooked out-of-state wholesale distributors, it is sometimes sold back to unsuspecting retailers who unwittingly buy back their own stolen merchandise, or someone else's. Criminal organizations responsible include South American, Mexican, and Cuban criminal groups, and Asian street gangs from California. In the words of Special Agent Eric Ives, of the FBI's Organized Retail Theft program operating out of Washington, D.C., "Organized retail theft is a gateway crime that often leads us to major crime rings that use the illicit proceeds to fund other crimes – such as organized crime activities, health care fraud, money laundering, and potentially even terrorism."

ORC can take many forms. They might operate crooked trucking companies that legitimately deliver and unload the goods you ordered, but then sneakily load other goods of yours (sometimes whole pallets of goods!) right out of your warehouse or stockroom into the back of their truck before they pull away from your loading dock. Sometimes they are responsible for all those problems you have with your suppliers— the mysterious discrepancies in what you ordered and what was delivered. Most often, ORC will sponsor professional shoplifting rings, which operate just like common shoplifting rings but with more sophisticated ways of fencing the stolen goods.

The following examples of ORC-related incidents show the enormity of the problem, whether it's the dollar amount involved, the length of time it went on, or the number of stores hurt by the thefts:

- Two unrelated cases occurred recently in the Kansas City, MO area. In one, $1,600 worth of Yankee candles was stolen from a Timeless Traditions store. In the second incident, three thieves stole around $100,000 in designer sunglasses from Vision Works and Lens Crafters stores in the Zona Rosa shopping district.
- In January 2013, West York Police (York County, PA) announced the arrest of more than 130 people. It included the leader of a major organized retail crime ring that targeted more than 90 stores at over 300 locations in five counties in Pennsylvania and two counties in northern Maryland.
- In Polk County, FL, eighteen people were arrested in an operation that targeted local department stores like Target and Wal-Mart, and then resold the items on eBay. Estimates over a five-year period put the amount stolen between $60 million and $100 million in merchandise.
- Another shoplifting ring, also broken up by the Polk County Sheriff's Department, operated for seven years and may have stolen as much as $17 million in baby formula.

How do you deal with a threat like this, one that's way above your pay grade?

I've already taught you 90% of what you need to know and do to combat ORC. After all, on your property, they will use the same methods any other shoplifters and thieves will use. The other 10% of your role in dealing with ORC may simply be your awareness that the sneakiest shoplifters could be part of something bigger than they appear— just one more reason to always call the police with detailed reports about those that got away, and do your best to apprehend and prosecute as many as you can, then let law enforcement use all that information to put the bigger picture together.

Every retailer who actively fights crime, and who reports any crime as it is noticed, is a huge help to local law enforcement and even the FBI. Our timely and accurate crime information gives them "data points" that would otherwise go unnoticed, helping them create a clearer picture of the tides, currents, and patterns of criminal activity. Here are a few practical ways you can minimize ORC activity in your store, neighborhood, or region:

Ways to combat ORC:

- Meet with your local police to find our what kind of merchandise is being targeted by organized crime in your area, to see if your store might be prone to these types of thefts. Let them know that you actively apprehend shoplifters, and you keep records —of successful apprehensions and of thieves that got away, and of suspected shoplifters that you are keeping an eye on— and that you would be happy to share your information and surveillance video with them.
- If criminal activity is increasing, arrange a quarterly or monthly meeting with a detective or watch commander to share information and concerns with them. At the very least, make sure that your regular crime reports contain all the information they want to track, and that they are being sent to the right person.
- Meet with other retailers in your area to compare notes about theft and other common crimes (like vandalism). Join a neighborhood council or your local chamber of

commerce. Find out what other local retailers are doing to fight shoplifting and other kinds of crime, and join them in their efforts. If nothing seems to be happening, pass along a copy of this book to them and begin a helpful discussion.

- Have camera systems operating at all times and have signage that alerts customers and potential thieves that their actions are being monitored. Even professional thieves want to avoid having their picture taken.
- Always try to get the license plate number of any getaway vehicle. Provide the police with your best possible description of any suspects, how the theft happened, what was stolen, and how many suspects were involved.

One Thing Remains Constant

Whichever of these shoplifter variations you run into, the guidelines for apprehending them remain the same. Nothing changes whether the thief is one of a group of teenagers, a drug addict, a professional con-artist, or someone involved in organized crime. Your safety and the safety of those around you is foremost, but you must also defend your livelihood. They are all just shoplifters stealing merchandise from your store, and with the exception of the armed smash-and-grab thieves, your job is to stop them! You do that by apprehending as many of them as you can as often as you can, working closely with the police (and other retailers), and following up with prosecution.

Chapter 9 – Prosecution Policy: You have options

Criminal Prosecution:

Every company, whether it's a big-name retailer or a stand-alone store, will have a different policy as to whether they file criminal charges against persons arrested for shoplifting. Your company, or you as the manager/business owner, will need to weigh the benefits versus the costs associated with the decision to prosecute.

The benefits should be obvious. You want to protect your store, your employees, and your assets (i.e. your investment in your business). Every shoplifter caught prevents further losses to your bottom line. And by fighting back against shoplifting, you are also supporting the other retailers in your immediate area as well as your local community. Since most crime is related, your efforts to fight shoplifting may reduce other crime in your area as well. Your employees will notice your efforts, and hopefully this will reduce any temptation for them to steal from you.

The costs to prosecute will include travel as well as the time spent attending court hearings and testifying as to what happened. Although it will take you away from the store, this is actually time well spent. If you are going to prosecute, then you have to be willing to attend any and all hearings to ensure the person you caught does not go unpunished. You may be the only witness to the crime. Your failure to appear in court could result in the charges being dropped. Another cost is the proper training associated with the surveillance and apprehension of a shoplifter. At CrimeFighters USA, this is our area of expertise. Rest assured that any costs associated with training, surveillance, apprehension and prosecution will receive a return on investment many times over.

Having a prosecution policy in writing is important for several reasons. It will clarify your expectations and standards for your employees, for training purposes. It will make processing shoplifters go more smoothly, especially if your own adrenaline and emotions are running high and you need to calm down and think clearly: your written policy represents decisions you made ahead of time with a clear head and plenty of time to think them through. As such, your written policy also protects you from accusations of prejudice and profiling, as long as you follow it with every person you apprehend. So, you will need to have a written prosecution policy, as well as some unwritten guidelines to go by. It can't just be based on gut feelings or the individual circumstances of each case, although those kinds of judgment calls might come into play occasionally.

The following are some guidelines that have been used by various retailers in determining whether to prosecute shoplifting cases. Each one in and of itself is a legitimate reason to prosecute a shoplifter. You may want to incorporate the declaration of intent and some or all of these policies as your own:

Prosecution Guidelines

Declaration of Intent: "We will prosecute a person apprehended for shoplifting (or any other kind of theft, burglary, vandalism, destruction of private property, disorderly conduct, trespassing, assault, or any other crime committed on our property) if they meet any of the following criteria:"

1. **No Identification – All persons apprehended by store personnel must be positively identified before releasing them from our custody.**
   Most people carry some sort of identification, usually a driver's license or student ID. Without proper ID, you cannot implement civil demand; in fact, you cannot be sure who they really are. In this case you need to call the police so they can identify the subject, even if you later decide not to press charges. Some persons will outright refuse to identify themselves until you convince them that unless they produce

something with their name and address on it, they are going to jail. In one example, finally convinced that I wasn't bluffing, the shoplifter called home, explained his circumstances, and pleaded with a family member to bring his identification to the store. We had a lot of shocked spouses whenever this happened. In another instance the subject, who had no ID on him, took us out to his car where he had recent mail with his name and address on it.

Always note the make, model, and license plate number of any car associated with a shoplifter so that you can trace the vehicle if their ID turns out to be phony.

2. **Refusal to Sign – The shoplifter refuses to sign an admission of wrongdoing.**
Every store I worked at required us to fill out an apprehension report whenever we caught a shoplifter. All of those reports had a statement section at the bottom for the shoplifter to sign, admitting responsibility for what happened in the store that day. I would explain our report to the shoplifter like this:
"Here is our security statement of what happened today. The top section has all of your personal information that you provided. The center section lists all the items that were taken and recovered, as well as the total dollar amount. The last section is a short paragraph with a space at the bottom for you to sign, that basically states you are accepting responsibility for your actions."
Then I would hand it to them and say, **"Sign here, please."**
Although a signed admission of wrongdoing carries little weight in court (your testimony, as the one who made the apprehension, is what counts), a suspect's refusal to sign may indicate several things. First of all, it may be simply that the suspect just won't sign anything (and they are not required to do so). Second, this person may have a problem with accepting responsibility for their actions. And finally, it may indicate they are going to fight this in court. So be it. You'll see them in court!
This particular guideline goes for adults only. Never have a juvenile shoplifter sign anything without a parent or legal guardian present.

3. **Resisting Arrest – Physical restraint and/or pursuit is required to return the shoplifter back into the store.**
If a shoplifter is resisting arrest, there is usually a good reason

why. Shoplifters who are repeat offenders do not want to get caught again. On the other hand, those are the thieves you most want to prosecute. In one instance, I chased a guy through the parking lot and across the highway, then wrestled him to the ground and held him down until the cops got there, all while being threatened by his friends. That was a long minute until I heard police sirens approaching. This guy simply did not want to get caught again. He had prior arrests, so he tried his best to escape. These particular thieves will push past you as you step in front of them to identify yourself. They will almost inevitably run. And up until you have gained control of them, they will resist your best efforts. These types of incidents, although being the most exciting in your memoirs some day, can also be the most dangerous. That's why you must be sure to prosecute whenever a shoplifter chooses to resist, especially if they resist so vigorously: they are likely to be the most active and, in time, the most dangerous thieves, and we must get them off the streets (and out of your aisles).

4. **Previous Arrests – The shoplifter has been arrested in this store previously, or has previous arrests or convictions for retail theft.**
The local police can run a background check to determine this for you. The "Salt & Pepper Bandit" apprehended in chapter eight almost walked right out of my office with only a citation, until I asked the accompanying officer to step outside with me to speak in private. Once I was out of the suspect's hearing range, I explained to the officer that the suspect was a career criminal that we had been trying to catch for a long time, and asked the officer to run a background check on him. The background check revealed several previous retail theft charges, as well as one for impersonating an officer. This shoplifter finally left my office, not walking out freely on his own, but in handcuffs, escorted by the officer past the checkout lines, past the customers, and straight to the police cruiser.

5. **High Dollar Loss – Total retail value of merchandise stolen, damaged, or lost is equal to or greater than** [*some non-trivial amount you set ahead of time that you believe ought to result in automatic prosecution: $50, $100, whatever you decide*].
Whenever a shoplifter steals something that a customer in

your store would have paid a lot of money for, prosecute them. If they did damage to the store, like breaking into a locked display case, add estimated damages to the total of the loss. They may be cooperative, sign your paperwork, have proper identification, and even have no prior arrests. But if you have a predetermined dollar amount that you have decided to use as a guideline to prosecute, and they steal more than that dollar amount, they've just made it easy for you to prosecute. In your store, if a person steals something expensive, send them to jail, no questions asked.

6. **Lack of Civil Demand – Our company does not utilize civil recovery rights and statutes.**
I recommend the use of civil demand (which I will explain later in this chapter), but if your company does not make use of civil demand, your options are limited. You will have to either release them or prosecute them. Make it a habit to prosecute them, or all your efforts will have been in vain.

Remember, all you really need is a good reason to call the police. Any of the above, or any combination of the above, is a good reason; please use them to come up with your own set of guidelines. I'm sure there are others you could add to this list. **Possession of illegal drugs** might be one. If they have drugs on them, the police need to know. **Lying to me** used to be another one. I didn't like it when someone lied to me. But after a while you begin to realize that if they steal from you, they're probably also going to lie about it to you. Expect it.

Grading of Offenses

Shoplifting offenses are normally graded by the dollar amount of the theft and the number of times the person has been arrested for this particular crime. Each rise in grade is a reflection of the seriousness of the offense. In the Pennsylvania Crimes Code it looks like this:

1) Summary Offense – Lowest level of seriousness. Reflects a low dollar amount or a first offense. It is similar to receiving a traffic citation.

2) Misdemeanor Offense – Middle level of seriousness. Reflects a high dollar amount or a second offense. A misdemeanor

offense can also be categorized as either 1st or 2nd degree, according to the circumstances of the crime.

3) Felony Offense – Highest level of seriousness. This offense can be for any dollar amount, as long as it is a third offense. It is categorized as a 3rd degree felony and carries the most severe penalties.

1st Offense

- If the first offense is less than $150, it is a summary offense.
- If the first offense is more than $150, it is a 1st degree misdemeanor.
- If the first offense is more than $2,000, it is a 3rd degree felony.

2nd Offense

- If the second offense is less than $150, it is a 2nd degree misdemeanor.
- If the second offense is more than $150, it is a 1st degree misdemeanor.
- If the second offense is more than $2,000, it is a 3rd degree felony.

3rd Offense

- For the third offense, it doesn't matter what the dollar amount is. In the State of Pennsylvania, this is automatically a 3rd degree felony.

Your state's criminal code may differ from Pennsylvania's, and you will want to familiarize yourself with the laws in your state, but this gives you an idea of what you can expect: first offenses are only mild ones if the value of the theft is relatively low, while repeat offenders quickly face felony charges even for relatively minor theft.

Prosecution – Why File Criminal Charges?

There are three areas of responsibility that obligate you to file criminal charges against shoplifters:

1) **To your employer** – If you fail to apprehend the shoplifter, and only recover your store's merchandise, the thief or thieves will most likely return to your store at another time when you are not there to prevent it. But once you have caught someone, your follow-up responsibility is to prevent them from coming back into your store. By successfully apprehending them and prosecuting them (by filing criminal charges), you can stop them from ever entering your store again. If they are warned by you or by the court not to enter your store, and they do come back in, it's now defiant trespassing. You can call the police immediately without waiting to observe a theft, have them escorted out of your store, and even prosecute them for defiant trespassing.

2) **To your local community** - By successfully apprehending and prosecuting a shoplifter, you have effectively taken a criminal off the streets. They will be less likely to continue their shoplifting ways or take any chance of being arrested again in your area, since they are now known to the local police. And since subsequent offenses are aggravated, the shoplifter is taking a bigger risk of increased penalties if they continue their criminal behavior. You have done your community, as well as other retailers in your area, a valuable service.

3) **To the shoplifter** – Yes, believe it or not, you also have a responsibility to the person you have just caught. For repeat offenders, criminal prosecution may be the only solution to stopping their theft problem, however much they don't want to hear that. But whether it's a repeat offender or a first-timer, I've had both beg me, "Please don't call the police!" As for me, as soon as I hear that request, I immediately pick up the phone and start dialing.
By "first-timer" I mean the first time they've been caught. They will all tell you the same story, that it's the first time they've ever done it. You'll get used to hearing that one.

Some people just need to get caught once and be so embarrassed by their actions that they never do it again. That is a true first-timer. First attempted theft and first time caught! After it's all said and done, the true first-timer may even thank you later (don't expect a thank you from the repeat offender). I have had several adults come back and thank me for what I did. Only by being ushered into the criminal justice system were they finally able to realize what their behavior was doing to them and their families.

Now as for juveniles caught shoplifting, they will also plead with you, with a slight variation that goes something like, "Please don't call my parents!" But if ever a juvenile offender needed parental guidance, it is now. And when dealing with a young offender, your responsibility to inform the family is critical. How you handle a juvenile can have a huge impact on them for the rest of their life. So make the call and get the parents involved as soon as possible.

Civil Demand

> *"Someone finally figured out how to have*
> *the shoplifters pay for the security in the*
> *stores!" – Anonymous*

An alternative to filing criminal charges against shoplifters apprehended in your store is the use of "civil demand" or "civil recovery." So far we've been talking about prosecuting shoplifters by having them arrested by the local police, and then filing criminal charges in your local jurisdiction. This method of justice and punishment, although effective, can be time consuming as well as a financial burden to you the merchant (not to mention the court system and the shoplifter). The use of civil demand or civil recovery (available in all fifty states under one of these names) gives you another option. Beginning in 1990, retailers in Pennsylvania were given the authority to apply civil demand to retail theft cases. The justice system finally came up with a way for the merchants to not only punish the shoplifters, but also recoup some of their financial losses by having fines (civil penalties) paid directly to them.

With every shoplifter apprehended, you have a decision to make. Once you've caught them, identified them, and recovered your merchandise, do you now call the police? And what determines that decision? Recall the prosecution guidelines given previously: no identification, refusing to sign the statement, resisting arrest, previous arrests for theft, and high dollar amount of the loss. If none of these apply, then they should be a candidate for civil demand.

Here's how civil demand should work: Instead of calling the police, you explain to the shoplifter that your company has another option available. In lieu of filing criminal charges against them, or having the police come right now and issue them a citation, a fine or civil penalty can be paid directly to the store. If the fine is not paid within a certain period of time, then criminal charges can still be filed. (Note: Double dipping—filing criminal charges *and* imposing a civil penalty—may be legal in some states, but it defeats the purpose of civil demand, which is to give you a different option.)

Explain that within the next ten days they will receive a letter in the mail. This letter will include an invoice for an amount equal to $150 (this base fine may differ in some states) plus the value of the merchandise taken. Even though the items were recovered and are able to be resold, the dollar amount of the pilfered items determines the amount of the fine that exceeds $150. Some individuals will have a tough time understanding why, if the merchandise was recovered and not damaged, their fine is more than $150. They have to understand that the amount of $150 is only the starting point. For example, if subject A takes a $10 item, her fine is $160. If subject B takes a $45 item, his fine is $195. Also, in most states, the civil penalty may not exceed $650 ($150 plus $500 in merchandise taken). I don't know of many cases where the fine is this large. If the dollar amount of merchandise taken is over $100, and certainly if it is over $500, you may want to fall back on criminal prosecution.

The letter they receive should also explain that the fine must be paid within a certain time frame, usually 30 days. (Do not take any payment on the spot!) If not paid by the due date, the shoplifter will still face possible criminal prosecution. It's usually a pretty good incentive to pay. If you are the shoplifter, why face being slapped with a criminal record when you can just pay the fine and be done with it? Some would argue that this is a form of extortion. Not at all: it's a legal fine for a crime they committed against us, a right given to us by the power of the state legislature. The shoplifter is simply given the opportunity to pay the civil penalty. If they choose not to, then they may face criminal charges. The choice is completely in their hands, just as it was with their decision to steal.

This is another reason why it is imperative to properly identify the subject. If you aren't able to positively identify them, and then decide to use civil demand, your civil demand letter will probably come back with "No Known Address" written across the top. And now in addition to getting away with his crime, the shoplifter has just made a fool of you! If the subject can't produce positive identification, in some jurisdictions you may be able to call the police just to come and identify them for you. Then again, if they have no identification, go back to your prosecution guidelines. Let the police handle it and file the charges. But be absolutely sure whenever you decide to prosecute anyone. In most jurisdictions, once filed, the courts are very reluctant to withdraw any criminal charges. You may not be able to go back and have civil demand as an option.

Issues Associated with Civil Demand

First time offenders only – Civil demand should not be offered to every shoplifter, only to first-time offenders. Once someone has been in the system and has one or more convictions for retail theft, civil demand is not a viable option. If you have a shoplifter with prior offenses, this person needs to face criminal prosecution again. The threat of having a criminal record thus far has not prevented them from going out and stealing once more. Paying a civil penalty certainly isn't going to stop them, either, and letting them go so you can pursue civil demand gives them an opportunity to hide from collection and prosecution. They need to go before a judge and pay some hefty fines, face jail time, or both. Some people will only learn the hard way.

Paperwork that explains civil demand – You will need a form letter that explains civil demand, or at least have copies of the state statute to hand out to anyone you are considering offering it to.

Companies that handle civil demand payments (3rd party) – There are companies out there that will handle the civil demand letter and subsequent payments for you. They may work on a commission basis or on a straight fee per case. Most of the larger retailers will use this method of collection.

Juvenile procedure: Every juvenile apprehended should be financially responsible for their actions, even if the parents have to pay the civil penalty. And parents need to be included in this decision. See Pennsylvania Crimes Code Section 8308 (b) relating to minors. There are plenty of ways that each young man or young lady can work to pay back (possibly with interest) the amount they now owe their parents. From cutting lawns to baby sitting, juveniles can earn the money to reimburse mom and dad. Convince the parents to be tough in this area.

In summary, with civil demand the shoplifter pays a civil penalty (a fine) directly to the merchant, and by doing so he or she may avoid entering the justice system. So, in addition to the merchants benefitting, the courts will also benefit by not being clogged with excessive retail theft cases to process. Not only is this a win-win situation for the merchant and the court system, but the shoplifter, if a first-timer, also benefits from the use of civil demand by paying a civil penalty and possibly avoiding a criminal record.

For those of you who are stand-alone merchants, my suggestion to you is to leave it to the big retailers to continue using civil demand, with all its issues and headaches. Unless you want to start running your own collection agency and chasing down those who refuse to pay, you have more important things to do, like managing your business.

Accelerated Rehabilitative Disposition (ARD)

One other option available for the Pennsylvania shoplifter is Accelerated Rehabilitative Disposition, or ARD. If the person qualifies, they may be admitted to the program. In order to qualify, the individual would have to be arrested for a non-violent crime such as shoplifting, and be a first-time offender. The program can include classroom time, community service and/or a fine. A period of probation is also usually assessed. If the program is completed successfully along with probation (with no additional criminal offenses), they may petition the court to have the charges dismissed and their record expunged. This option gives the shoplifter the opportunity to maintain a clean record, with no criminal conviction. There are county-by-county differences in Pennsylvania and surely in your state as well, so check your particular jurisdiction to see if they offer this kind of program.

Until now, we have been discussing shoplifters and the decisions you must make as to whether or not to prosecute them for their actions. But what do you do when you catch an *employee* stealing? What options are available to you? In the next chapter we will discuss dishonest employees and how best to handle them.

Chapter 10 – Internal Theft

Every store owner or manager who has experienced employee theft realizes the breach of trust that has occurred. You expect some theft from the public at large, but when it's your own employees, some who have been trusted for years, who are stealing from you, anguish, frustration, and disgust will naturally result. The following definition provides a little more detail into this desperate criminal activity.

> ***Employee Theft:*** The unauthorized taking, control, or transfer of money and/or property of the formal work organization, perpetrated by an employee during the course of occupational activity which is related to his or her employment. (*Merriam Dictionary* 1977)

It may be simple to define, but it's a lot harder to discover and eliminate.

Shoplifters vs. Dishonest Employees

Internal theft is just another form of shoplifting, except that it's from your employees. However, there is a key difference between shoplifters and dishonest employees to keep in mind. Shoplifters may be regular customers who only come into your store on a weekly basis and steal occasionally, but they're only there for a limited amount of time. They may be able to pick you out (the plain clothes detective) and get to know a few aisles in the store that are good to steal from, but that's about it. But with employees, there is a lot more familiarity. They work with you; they know you. They get to know one another, everyone else who works for you, and often your vendors and distributors. And because of the time they spend in the store, they become familiar with your store policies and procedures, with your store's routines and strengths… and also its weaknesses.

Steps in an Internal Theft Investigation

1. Discovery: The initial discovery or exposing of internal theft; the realization that these losses are not caused by an outside agency like shoplifters, loading-dock thieves, or crooked vendors/distributors. It must have been "an inside job." This discovery may be the result of regular audits of company procedure or a random surveillance from a concealed camera. Most of the time though, it comes from a tip, and usually from another employee.
2. Investigation: Gathering evidence, whether visual (via a stake out), physical, personal, electronic, or video, to find the source of the losses and make your case. Surveillance of the suspect's activities becomes paramount.
3. Apprehension: If an employee walks out of the store with unpaid-for merchandise, you can apprehend them just like a shoplifter.
4. Interrogation: An interview similar to the one you use to process a shoplifter, but with additional things to consider, which may vary by state.
5. Recovery: This occurs either through restitution or recovery of the actual stolen merchandise. In one case, once we got an admission, the dishonest employee gave us permission to go to that employee's home and retrieve what she had stolen. We recovered several shopping bags full of new, never-worn clothing with price tags from our store still attached. More detail will follow on this case later in the chapter.

Investigation

It is often tempting for sole proprietors of small retail businesses to skip this step and go straight from Discovery to Apprehension. This is a huge mistake, and can cost you much more that the amount you may already have lost, particularly in states like New York, Illinois, and California where labor laws strongly support the employee in cases of unmerited accusation of wrongdoing, especially when the employee is fired on that basis, or when criminal charges are filed.

Just as you must witness the theft so as not to make a bad stop of a shoplifter, you must have more than merely circumstantial evidence before you confront an employee with any accusation of criminal wrongdoing. In the process, you will make sure that you have the right suspect, and hopefully discover accomplices if there are any. Of course, just as with shoplifters, the best substantial evidence is witnessing the illegal act yourself, or recording it clearly on video. But building a case with other kinds of evidence, both substantial and circumstantial, is always a good idea.

If you feel you lack the instincts or expertise to craft and carry out an investigation, or the tools to do it properly, you can hire a loss-prevention specialist to handle the investigation for you. Before you do, please call or email me for a free consultation: in most cases you will be able to handle it yourself. You do not need to go to detective school to discover and investigate internal theft or fraud. The variety of approaches already available to you may surprise you.

Discovery and Investigative Tools at Your Disposal

1. Cash shortage tracking – In a larger store where multiple employees will ring up purchases on multiple registers, you need a way to track those shortages and the people who work those registers. A simple diagram similar to the one in Appendix B will help you do this.
2. Bag checks – Inspect all employee purchases at the end of their work shift. You can do a spot check now and then, or make it mandatory for everyone always.
3. Honesty Shopping – All new employees should be "honesty shopped." This happens as they are running the cash register and are given opportunities to prove their integrity without realizing they are being tested. One test involves undercover shoppers bringing items to the register to purchase, to see whether they are rung up at the correct price. Some of the items may have their price falsely altered, or one item may be concealed inside a second item. Another test has the undercover shopper pretending to be in a hurry and "accidentally" leaving the correct amount of cash on the counter along with the price tag or ticket of a clothing item they have taken with them, perhaps a sweater. Unbeknownst to the cashier, they are being watched to see whether they ring up the sweater or pocket the cash instead.
4. CCTV – Surveillance cameras should be installed in all sensitive areas, above every cash register, as well as all entrance and exit doors.

5. Tips from other associates – probably your most valuable tool. Cultivate the trust and loyalty of every person who works with you.

Apprehension

In most cases, once an investigation has given indisputable proof or direct observation of the theft, the dishonest employee is asked to report to your office while still on the clock, before they have left for the day, so that you can confront them with your evidence in an interrogative interview. If you have carried out your Discovery and Investigation discreetly, the employee will not suspect that their illegal activity has been noticed, and you will have no trouble having them simply report to your office during their shift.

If a dishonest employee does suspect they are about to be caught, they may suddenly become scarce. When you are ready to confront them and they are taking sick days or an unexpected vacation etc., or simply not showing up for work, do not hesitate to call the police and explain the situation to them. Of course, this could mean filing criminal charges immediately, which might have been delayed or even avoided if they had made themselves available for your interview and confrontation.

Interrogation

The following scenario is a step-by-step interview-and-confrontation process used by a former retail chain. You may not feel you have the expertise to craft and carry out an investigation, or all of the tools to do it properly, but with practice you can handle the interview and confrontation with confidence. Adapt and rehearse the following interrogation process, which I have successfully used in the past.

Preparation

Once you have done your homework and concluded your investigation, it's time to wrap it all up. At this point, you should be certain as to the guilt of the suspect. You may have video evidence to back up your findings. You must have *some* kind of convincing substantial evidence, or your investigation is still inconclusive! Once you do, it's time to interview the suspect and confront them with your findings. The unfriendly but proper name for this is "Interrogation." I'll use the common term "Interview" here: it's important to handle this as graciously as the suspect will allow, and always maintain a professional and controlled demeanor, so if thinking of it as an "interview" will help you avoid slipping into "interrogator mode," then do so.

Finding the right words to say can be very difficult as you interview an employee, especially one you know personally, and who knows you. Because of this, I am including a detailed and annotated script that takes you through the heart of the Interview process. Rehearse the key portions of the Interview script in language that feels natural to you so you can speak them while watching the associate's face and body language, instead of reading your explanations and questions straight out of this book, or off a cue sheet (although if you need a cue sheet to help you remember every step, and to help you get back on track if you are distracted, by all means make one for yourself). Invite the associate into your office, or someplace private but not isolated (see Chapter 5, Obtain a Witness, and do so if you have any concern about possible retaliation). Show them to a chair across from your desk. Provide a sturdy solid armchair if available—one they can't fidget in or move around in very much. Have your evidence ready to present at the appropriate moment.

Interview

Step 1 – Start by telling the associate, *We are here today to discuss company business.* Begin with what Loss Prevention does, saying: *Our responsibility is to prevent and minimize the loss of company assets. Among other things, those assets include:*
1) *The building and furnishings*
2) *The cash*
3) *The merchandise*
4) *And the most important asset: our employees.*

Explain to them, *My job with loss prevention is to investigate any type of loss incurred by the store. These losses might be:*
1) *External Losses – Shoplifting, bad checks, and credit card fraud*
2) *Safety Related – Workers' comp cases and customer accidents*

3) *Internal Losses – Caused by employee theft of cash or merchandise*

We have different ways we protect those assets, like:
1) *The use of an undercover operative*
2) *Honesty shops*
3) *Register audits*
4) *The use of video surveillance – to be 100% sure.*

Through the use of video surveillance, just like **this** (at this time you pull out a physical copy of the video surveillance evidence and lay it on the desk, making the idea concrete) *we gather evidence necessary to prove our case in court.* If your strongest evidence is something different, like the personal witness of an undercover operative, then lay that report on the table instead and talk about undercover surveillance.

Step 2 – Explain the investigation process.
Once we determine there is a problem, we begin to conduct an investigation, starting with a background check. You'd be surprised how many people falsify information on an application. We then review all of the information gathered from the tools mentioned previously. We review:
1) *What the losses were,*
2) *When and where the losses occurred*
3) *Who is causing it and how it's being done*
4) *How can we prevent the same losses from happening in the future*

Once the investigation is concluded, we prepare our case for the district attorney's office. But before any charges are filed or anyone is arrested, we put a hold on everything. We do this because we realize that people make mistakes. They do so for different reasons: peer pressure, problems at home or in marriage, financial issues — car payments due, child support, etc. — and possibly drug or alcohol problems. In every case, there usually is some underlying problem.

Step 3 – Make it personal. *We have recently concluded an investigation in the department you work in, and have found that mistakes were made here at this store, mistakes in judgment. We have the facts we need. Now we want to know the why. Keeping in mind all of what I've just talked about, there's another reason I asked you here today, and that's to talk about the mistakes you've made. We only ask a few things:*

    1) Do you want my help?

    2) Are you willing to give me your 100% honesty and cooperation?

After the employee answers both of these questions affirmatively, you can then proceed to the crux of the matter. If the employee is already hostile and defensive, the rest of this script will still give you helpful language and terms to use, and talking points you must be sure to cover in one way or another. If you have reason to expect belligerence, I offer a more detailed contingency tree on my website.

Introduce your loaded question: *Do you know what a "loaded question" is? It's a question I already know the answer to. I can't stress enough the importance of your honesty and cooperation right now in answering my questions from this point on.* (Use their name when asking this next question)

[John/Jennifer], when was the last time you were responsible for a loss of assets to the company?

Often they will remain silent for a moment, or say they don't understand. Let them sit with the question a bit while you describe two different directions the rest of the interview will go: *I want you to think about that.*

There are two types of people I meet in this situation.

    The first type doesn't want my help. They're arrogant and in self-denial. They've also "never made any mistakes" even though my investigation shows differently.

    The second type wants to do the right thing and get these problems cleared up!

Now, we are willing to go the extra mile and are willing to work with you. All we ask is 100% honesty and cooperation.

At this time I will repeat the question, **When was the last time you were responsible for a loss of assets to the company?** (It is best to use your own company name.)

One of two things will happen at this point. First, since you have now properly motivated the associate, they should be more than willing to confess and admit to all of their wrongdoing. As you were talking, you should have been able to see signs of their discomfort, like not maintaining eye contact, or fidgeting in their chair. It may not be easy for them to admit what they have done, but as they slowly do, ask them questions for more detail, and always encourage them to *"please continue."*

The second thing that can happen is that they go into denial. If there is a negative response and they opt to deny any wrongdoing, you will have to be more convincing. The following statements can be helpful whenever this occurs:
- *You must believe we are trying to help you.*
- *No matter how much you want to change what's happened, you can't go back.*
- *We already know who is responsible. Right now you are making decisions that will affect your career and possibly your life.*

It's possible they may not admit to anything. There are some who will never admit to wrongdoing no matter what you say. That is, unless you prove it to them. This is the time when you play the video and show them your evidence. You never want to go into an interview bluffing or on a fishing trip. You do not want to throw your fishing line in during the interview and only *hope* to catch a big fish. You want to already have that fish on the line. All you want to have to do in the interview is reel it in! Once they see themselves on video, it should be easy to get a confession.

There will also be some situations where you have the dishonest associate caught red-handed. One is when they walk out with unpaid-for store merchandise, just like a shoplifter. There can be no denial here. So go ahead and process them just like a shoplifter, except add one more step: get them to admit to previous thefts with an interview like this one.

Step 4 – <u>Produce a written record</u>. Once they have admitted to you what they have done, you can now have them complete a written statement detailing all of their unlawful activities while employed by your company. Explain to them that this written record is to help them remember everything. Make sure you have them give as much detail as possible and explain each item listed. Have them include dates if they can recall them. And if you know there is more than what they write down, you can say, *"It's what you don't*

put down that tells me you're not being totally honest with me."
When they have completed the statement and you are satisfied,
have them sign and date it.

It goes without saying that you should always have one person of
the same sex as the employee present at all times during the
interview. Both of you may walk out of the room to leave the
suspect alone as they begin to fill out the statement, but leave the
door open so you can visually monitor them. Quietly spiteful
vandalism, records tampering, or petty theft could be the least of
your worries. In one instance, a male employee was left alone to
complete his statement. When we walked back into the office, he
had cut himself on both of his arms several times. It was only
scratches, nothing serious. It may have been self-punishment, or it
may have been the beginning of a false accusation of assault. You
don't want any surprises, so have someone maintain visual contact
even if you leave the room.

Recovery

As usual, your ultimate goal is not just to catch thieves but to
recover what has been stolen, as much as possible anyway. This
can involve recovering the stolen merchandise in salable
condition, or recovering the value of the stolen merchandise
through restitution, or both. Recovery does not always go so
easily. Even though you have the dishonest employee in your
custody, with a case against them that will stand up in court, and
have done your best to get them to understand the seriousness of
their actions, to express remorse and to confess in detail and in
writing (it might be your handwriting or typing, but it is their
signature, if they have cooperated), you still may not fully recoup
your losses. You must pursue every avenue of recovery.
You might turn them over to the police and file criminal charges,
hoping to recover damages through the courts. Or you might
pursue civil demand as a means of recouping some of your losses.
Sometimes, just getting rid of a dirty associate is enough of a
victory.

Examples of Internal Theft Cases (and How They Were Solved)

1) **Cleaning Crew Associate** – We routinely audited our vending machines in the store. One particular machine kept coming up short. During the interview, after questioning a member of the cleaning crew who happened to be the only person to have access to this machine, I then laid five coins on the desk. The total of the coins was the exact amount missing from the machine. As soon as I laid the coins down, he confessed! It wasn't the dollar amount that was important here, but the use of physical evidence that caused the employee to admit his dishonesty.

2) **Dishonest Cashier** – An 18-year-old sales associate got an idea for a way to have some of the nice clothing they sell in the store without paying for it. For her, it started with the question, "How can I make it look like it's been purchased and not stolen?" All she had to do was ring up a sale when no one was around, just to produce the receipt. Of course she couldn't pay for the item, so to ensure her register wasn't short, she rang up a refund for the same amount. This balanced her register and gave her a receipt that she could now place in a bag along with the item she wanted. However, she didn't count on someone monitoring the excessive refunds coming from her register. Once we placed a camera up in the ceiling above her register, we were able to observe her scheme. We brought her into the office, interviewed her and confronted her with the evidence. She confessed to committing this refund scam for an extended period of time. Shortly after the interview, we drove out to her residence, and with her permission entered the house and came out with four garbage bags full of women's clothing. The total amount recovered was worth almost $1,500.00.

3) **Snack Bar Associate** – a 45-year-old cafeteria associate got away with theft for far too long. Credit for catching this one goes to the store manager who knew that all of the stores in the district had a profitable cafeteria, except his. He couldn't figure out why, so on his suspicion, we put up a camera. It didn't take long to find out where the profits were going. We soon gathered evidence on videotape of this associate taking cash from the register. We actually got her on tape twice to make sure we had her. She confessed rather easily once

confronted with the evidence. By the time the interview was over, she had admitted to stealing over $4,500.00 in cash and food items over a two-year period. No wonder this particular cafeteria couldn't show a profit!

4) **Housewares Associate** – A young woman made it a habit of helping herself to everyday store merchandise. Taking things like cleaning products, food items and kitchen utensils became routine for her. Another associate provided us with the tip we needed to put a stop to her "shopping sprees." The associate in question would begin her day by placing an empty box on her work cart. Throughout the day, as she was stocking shelves, she would place items she wanted into the box. At the end of the day, she would carry the box over and place it near the time clock with either her smock or a bag over it. She thought she was smart because she always checked on which members of security were in before she would attempt to take anything out of the store. In fact, she would always wait until I went to lunch. Then she would just walk out with her box of items after clocking out. So, in order to catch her, we had to make her believe I was out to lunch. Again, we didn't have to wait long.

Within a few days she began to fill up another box. I had an office on the sales floor near the Toy Department. At lunchtime I entered my office and left the door slightly open to make it clear that I was in there. But instead of having a sandwich, I was on the phone with one of my detectives who was monitoring her movements with binoculars from a perch on the back wall. He kept me informed (via a store phone) of everywhere she went, including when she walked past my office to make sure I was in there. The office manager, who was also assisting us, already informed me there was a box of merchandise once again near the time clock. She also verified that there had been no employee purchases that day. This associate, feeling confident that security was out to lunch, went for it!

Now, I had to remain in there until the last possible moment. My detective in the perch told me she had entered the time clock area, and then had exited with the box in hand. It was time for me to make my move. I left my office, running past the registers to the front doors. I got there a little too soon because as I rounded the corner she was just exiting through the foyer, and saw me. But, apparently feeling very confident, she continued out the doors into the parking lot. I apprehended her, just like a shoplifter, before she could make it to her car. In this particular case the dollar amount recovered was small. The contents of the box were less than $50.00, although we did get her to admit to previous thefts. What this particular case displays is the ingenuity and teamwork involved in outsmarting a dishonest associate. This was before any camera system was installed in the store. We didn't even have radios; we had to use in-store phones to communicate. In this case a simple bag/package check would have prevented this one from occurring. It shows the need to have policies and procedures in place so that employees aren't tempted to try things like this.

Cash Register Shortages

It's a common occurrence. When balancing a cash register at the end of the day, its inevitable that the cash won't always match the receipts. When it occurs on a regular basis, you realize you have a problem. Anytime you have register shortages, you need a way to track those shortages and to track the people who work those registers. The shortages chart (see appendix), using an Excel spreadsheet, is a simple way to identify who may be responsible for your cash losses. The two columns across the top track two items of information: the amount of the shortage or overage, and the date it occurred. The column on the left lists all of your associates who ring up customers on your registers. As you can see by the dollar amounts listed, sometimes a shortage will offset with an overage the next day. These ones you can ignore. In this particular example we plotted all shortages for the month of December. If a person worked on that day, they get an X underneath that day across from their name. If there is one person responsible for all of your shortages, his or her name will have an X under every day there is a shortage. That's your probable suspect. I say "probable" because if someone in your cash office is responsible for the losses, they could easily manipulate the shortage to implicate whomever they choose, or make it appear random. However, in most cases, the line of X's points to only one person. Now get a camera up and start recording!

Another Type of Insider Theft

We've looked at examples of *employee* theft in the workplace, but there is one area we have not explored. What happens when *upper management* is involved in dishonest practices? Sometimes a company can find itself in such financial trouble that senior executives succumb to whatever can be done to keep the ship afloat. The pressure these executives place on their management staff literally has them committing fraud. You can call it improving the bottom line, staying in the black, or making the company appear profitable on its tax return, but anyway you phrase it, it's all still fraud.

One company I worked for, which is no longer in business and will remain nameless, found itself in just such a dilemma. A couple of tricks they came up with included claiming excessive zero markdowns and moving merchandise from one store to another. Let's examine both, as well as their reasons for attempting these practices.

In the first instance, claiming excessive markdowns, there were items (coffee makers in this case) being marked down to zero and then being destroyed. They may have been defective or damaged returns. What mattered was, no matter how many coffee makers there were, I was told to sign off on paperwork claiming double that amount. If there were ten coffee makers being marked down to zero, I was expected to sign off on twenty. It was one practice the company started using to cover each store's shrinkage, but it had never before on my watch. I still recall the discussion the manager and I had at the time, as he sneered, "You didn't know the company takes unauthorized markdowns? You're getting awful picky now, aren't you?" I replied that there was no way my signature was going to appear on that paperwork. I refused to sign that one and I refused to sign any others after that.

In the second instance, also with the same company, security personnel along with all members of management were directed to load trucks with as much inventory as they could and ship it to another store in the district. Once that store received a shipment, it was then directed to send a similar shipment to a third store. This practice continued for months until the company was eventually bought out.

One immediate concern was the use of security personnel to perform the packing up of merchandise to ship, instead of allowing them to conduct their security duties. Obviously, these regular duties were deemed no longer necessary. This new practice soon became a daily responsibility, with the security managers moving from store to store as a team, depending which store was next in line to move merchandise.

Another alarming concern was store management's involvement, never questioning the practice. It's possible that, during that time, holding onto one's job was more important than being a whistleblower about something that may have seemed idiotic or even unethical but not "criminal." Their complacency in the continuation of this senseless practice soon became company policy, a policy that originated from upper management. One possible reason for this practice was to reduce the inventory of each store for accounting purposes by making sure there was always a lot of merchandise in transit (technically removing it from the books while it was en route... and making sure that a lot of inventory was endlessly en route).

Whatever the reason, I didn't stick around to find out. I saw the handwriting on the wall and knew the company was in trouble. It wasn't long after they adopted this practice that I left them to work for another retailer and the troubled company was bought out soon afterwards. The point to remember here is: dishonesty in retail is not confined to shoplifters or even employee theft. Sometimes circumstances can corrupt the person who signs your paycheck!

What do you do when company policy dictates that you perform any type of dishonest act? Going along with a sketchy scheme, even though it may be "for the good of the company," could end up with you being held liable. Your conscience will certainly hold you liable! Going along with officially sanctioned fraud sucks the heart out of your crimefighting work. Always say No!

A Comprehensive Plan – of Action!

If you are in the retail business for any length of time, you will most likely experience many of the various types of retail theft described in this book, from casual shoplifters to professional thieves, from dishonest employees to corrupt management, perhaps even organized crime. Some things you can fight directly (shoplifting and employee theft), some things you can only help law enforcement to fight, at least in your own small way (organized crime), and some things you must simply refuse to participate in (corrupt management practices). Appropriate responses to all of these require forethought and preparation. You have already taken the first step, by purchasing and reading this book. Now you have in your hands a set of proven principles, strategies and tactics to fight each one of these battles.

Budgeting Your Time and Money

To paraphrase a former U.S. Secretary of Defense, "You go into battle with the resources you have, not the resources you wish you had."[*] This diagram gives you a general idea of how you might invest your time and money, to varying degrees, to equip your business for the battle against retail theft:

Diagram #7

Time and Money

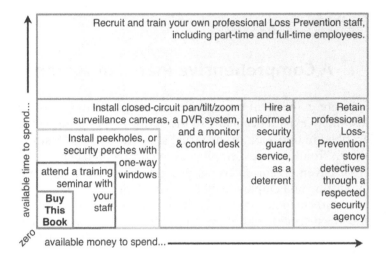

Despite all the technology out there and all its ever-changing upgrades, one aspect of Loss Prevention that has not changed and will not change is the hands-on apprehension of the shoplifter. Whether a concealment of merchandise is observed from a window perch through one-way glass, or from a pan/tilt/zoom camera system, someone still has to follow the shoplifter outside and stop them. The tools I have entrusted to you will give you the edge you need, not only to confront the shoplifters, but to bring them back inside with your merchandise, and prosecute them so it won't happen again! With every shoplifter you stop, your confidence will increase. You'll make mistakes, too. But with every mistake, you will learn what works better for the next time.

I have decided that this is my battle to fight. Is it yours as well?

What can you do? For your company, the local community and even the shoplifter? You may not think of yourself as a hero, but to the parent of a troubled teen you apprehend, you may be more than a hero. You can be the one who made an impression on their kid and turned his or her life around. To the local police you can be an asset, catching the thieves they *never* see, and giving them data to discover patterns they *need* to see. To the neighboring community and other businesses nearby, you can be the catalyst to clean up the neighborhood, so to speak, making their community safer to live in and shop in.

Any step you take toward implementing the principles in this book is a step in the right direction. Every step matters. Please, join me and thousands of other retail owners and managers in the continuing fight against the crime of retail theft.

---

[*] Donald Rumsfeld, CNN interview, December 8th 2004. Accessed August 2015. http://www.cnn.com/2004/US/12/08/rumsfeld.kuwait/index.html

About the Author

Vic Sellers is founder and chief loss prevention consultant for CrimeFighters USA. This retail theft prevention consulting and training business offers real-world experience to business owners who want to identify and fight the crime that affects their livelihood. Based in Western Pennsylvania, Mr. Sellers brings eighteen years of experience with major retailers including Wal-Mart and JC Penney. His well-honed techniques in retail theft prevention are proven by a career total of apprehending over eight hundred shoplifters and dishonest employees. Mr. Sellers teaches seminars, speaks at conferences, and offers one-on-one training for all who want to sharpen their loss-prevention skills and protect their store merchandise.

CrimeFighters USA gets results for retailers who must balance the needs of loss prevention with the concerns of budgetary constraints. For more information, go to CrimeFightersUSA.com.

Appendix A: Sample Apprehension Form

Apprehension Report

Miranda Warning:
You have the right to remain silent and make no statement at all.
Anything you say can and may be used against you in a court of law.
You have the right to talk to a lawyer and have him/her with you while you are being questioned.
If you cannot afford to hire a lawyer and if you wish one, you can request and receive appointment of a lawyer by the proper authority without cost or charge to you, to be present and to advise and to represent you before any questioning.

SIGNED:

CASE #_____STORE:_____DATE: _____

NAME:_____
        (Last)   (First)
    (Parent or Guardian)

ADDRESS:_____
    (Street) (City)   (State & Zip Code)

D.O.B.:_____AGE:___SEX:___PHONE:_____

PARENTS CALLED:__ARRIVED:____POLICE:_____

ITEM DESCRIPTION	**COST**	**QUANTITY**	**TOTAL**
1.			
2.			
3.			
4.			

Total $ Value Stolen:
Names of Witnesses:

X_____X_____

Appendix B: Sample Cash Register Spreadsheet

Cash Register Shortage Tracker

NAME:	1-Sep	4-Sep	5-Sep	7-Sep	9-Sep	13-Sep	16-Sep	20-Sep	23-Sep	24-Sep	28-Sep	30-Sep
Heather		X	X	X			X		X	X		X
Allison	X	X		X	X			X	X		X	
Nick	X		X		X			X		X		
Karen				X		X			X	X		
Joanne	X		X			X					X	X
James		X			X	X		X				X
Sandra		X	X				X	X			X	X
Elaine	X	X	X	X	X	X	X	X	X	X	X	X
Paula		X		X		X		X			X	
Frank	X		X				X		X			X
Robert		X	X			X		X	X			
Mary	X	X			X	X				X		X
Arnold			X	X			X	X	X			

Appendix C: One State's Criminal Code

Pennsylvania Crimes Code § 3929. Retail theft.

(a) Offense defined. A person is guilty of a retail theft if he:

(1)takes possession of, carries away, transfers or causes to be carried away or transferred, any merchandise displayed, held, stored or offered for sale by any store or other retail mercantile establishment with the intention of depriving the merchant of the possession, use or benefit of such merchandise without paying the full retail value thereof;

(2)alters, transfers or removes any label, price tag marking, indicia of value or any other markings which aid in determining value affixed to any merchandise displayed, held, stored or offered for sale in a store or other retail mercantile establishment and attempts to purchase such merchandise personally or in consort with another at less than the full retail value with the intention of depriving the merchant of the full retail value of such merchandise;

(3)transfers any merchandise displayed, held, stored or offered for sale by any store or other retail mercantile establishment from the container in or on which the same shall be displayed to any other container with intent to deprive the merchant of all or some part of the full retail value thereof; or

(4)under-rings with the intention of depriving the merchant of the full retail value of the merchandise.

(5)destroys, removes, renders inoperative or deactivates any inventory control tag, security strip or any other mechanism designed or employed to prevent an offense under this section with the intention of depriving the merchant of the possession, use or benefit of such merchandise without paying the full retail value thereof.

(b) Grading.

(1) Retail theft constitutes a:

(i) summary offense when the offense is a first offense and the value of the merchandise is less than $150.

(ii) misdemeanor of the second degree when the offense is a second offense and the value of the merchandise is less than $150.

(iii) misdemeanor of the first degree when the offense is a first or second offense and the value of the merchandise is $150 or more.

(iv) felony of the third degree when the offense is a third or subsequent offense, regardless of the value of the merchandise.

(v) felony of the third degree when the amount involved exceeds $1,000 or if the merchandise involved is a firearm or a motor vehicle.

(1.1) Any person who is convicted under subsection (a) of retail theft of motor fuel may, in addition to any other penalty imposed, be sentenced as follows:

(i) For a first offense, to pay a fine of not less than $100 nor more than $250.

(ii) For a second offense, to pay a fine of not less than $250 nor more than $500.

(iii) For a third or subsequent offense, to pay a fine of not less than $500, or the court may order the operating privilege of the person suspended for 30 days. A copy of the order shall be transmitted to the Department of Transportation.

(2)Amounts involved in retail thefts committed pursuant to one scheme or course of conduct, whether from the same store or retail mercantile establishment or several stores or retail mercantile establishments, may be aggregated in determining the grade of the offense.

(b.1)Calculation of prior offenses. For the purposes of this section, in determining whether an offense is a first, second, third or subsequent offense, the court shall include a conviction, acceptance of accelerated rehabilitative disposition or other form of preliminary disposition, occurring before the sentencing on the present violation, for an offense under this section, an offense substantially similar to an offense under this section or under the prior laws of this Commonwealth or a similar offense under the statutes of any other state or of the United States.

(c)Presumptions. Any person intentionally concealing unpurchased property of any store or other mercantile establishment, either on the premises or outside the premises of such store, shall be prima facie presumed to have so concealed such property with the intention of depriving the merchant of the possession, use or benefit of such merchandise without paying the full retail value thereof within the meaning of subsection (a), and the finding of such unpurchased property concealed, upon the person or among the belongings of such person, shall be prima facie evidence of intentional concealment, and, if such person conceals, or causes to be concealed, such unpurchased property, upon the person or among the belongings of another, such fact shall also be prima facie evidence of intentional concealment on the part of the person so concealing such property.

(c.1)Evidence. To the extent that there is other competent evidence to substantiate the offense, the conviction shall not be avoided because the prosecution cannot produce the stolen merchandise.

(d)Detention. A peace officer, merchant or merchant's employee or an agent under contract with a merchant, who has probable cause to believe that retail theft has occurred or is occurring on or about a store or other retail mercantile establishment and who has probable cause to believe that a specific person has committed or is committing the retail theft may detain the suspect in a reasonable manner for a reasonable time on or off the premises for all or any of the following purposes: to require the suspect to identify himself, to verify such identification, to determine whether such suspect has in his possession unpurchased merchandise taken from the mercantile establishment and, if so, to recover such merchandise, to inform a peace officer, or to institute criminal proceedings against the suspect. Such detention shall not impose civil or criminal liability upon the peace officer, merchant, employee, or agent so detaining.

(e)Reduction prohibited. No magisterial district judge shall have the power to reduce any other charge of theft to a charge of retail theft as defined in this section.

(f)Definitions.

"Conceal." To conceal merchandise so that, although there may be some notice of its presence, it is not visible through ordinary observation.

"Full retail value." The merchant's stated or advertised price of the merchandise.

"Merchandise." Any goods, chattels, foodstuffs or wares of any type and description, regardless of the value thereof.

"Merchant." An owner or operator of any retail mercantile establishment or any agent, employee, lessee, consignee, officer, director, franchisee or independent contractor of such owner or operator.

"Premises of a retail mercantile establishment." Includes but is not limited to, the retail mercantile establishment, any common use areas in shopping centers and all parking areas set aside by a merchant or on behalf of a merchant for the parking of vehicles for the convenience of the patrons of such retail mercantile establishment.

"Store or other retail mercantile establishment." A place where merchandise is displayed, held, stored or sold or offered to the public for sale.

"Under-ring." To cause the cash register or other sales recording device to reflect less than the full retail value of the merchandise.

(g) Fingerprinting. Prior to the commencement of trial or entry of plea of a defendant 16 years of age or older accused of the summary offense of retail theft, the issuing authority shall order the defendant to submit within five days of such order for fingerprinting by the municipal police of the jurisdiction in which the offense allegedly was committed or the State Police. Fingerprints so obtained shall be forwarded immediately to the Pennsylvania State Police for determination as to whether or not the defendant previously has been convicted of the offense of retail theft. The results of such determination shall be forwarded to the Police Department obtaining the fingerprints if such department is the prosecutor, or to the issuing authority if the prosecutor is other than a police officer. The issuing authority shall not proceed with the trial or plea in summary cases until in receipt of the determination made by the State Police. The magisterial district judge shall use the information obtained solely for the purpose of grading the offense pursuant to subsection (b).

(Dec. 2, 1976, P.L.1230, No.272, eff. imd.; Apr. 28, 1978, P.L.202, No.53, eff. 2 years; Dec. 20, 1996, P.L.1530, No.200, eff. 60 days; June 25, 1997, P.L.377, No.42, eff. imd.; Oct. 2, 2002, P.L.806, No.116, eff. 60 days; Nov. 30, 2004, P.L.1618, No.207, eff. 60 days; Dec. 23, 2013, P.L.1264, No.131, eff. 60 days)

2013 Amendment. Act 131 amended subsec. (b)(1)(v) and added subsec. (b.1). Section 3 of Act 131 provided that the amendment of subsec. (b)(1)(v) shall apply to offenses committed on or after the effective date of section 3. Section 4 of Act 131 provided that subsec. (b.1) shall apply to sentences imposed on or after the effective date of section 4.

2004 Amendment. Act 207 amended subsecs. (e) and (g). See section 29 of Act 207 in the appendix to this title for special provisions relating to construction of law.

2002 Amendment. Act 116 amended subsec. (b).

1997 Amendment. Act 42 added subsec. (a)(5).

Cross References. Section 3929 is referred to in sections 3903, 3929.2, 3929.3, 9112 of this title; sections 3573, 5552, 8308 of Title 42 (Judiciary and Judicial Procedure).

Made in the USA
Middletown, DE
10 January 2021